Scared of the Dark

Sean Felton

New Generation **Publishing**

Introduction

The first moment that you see and hold your child is magical – and unforgettable. As their eyes beam up at you, all full of innocence and need, you find yourself overcome with love, pride and an overwhelming need to protect. My son, Joe to me, was born on the 26th July 2007. His birth gave me a renewed sense of purpose and brought new-found joy and delight to my life. Two and a half years later, he was cruelly taken away from me. I had no warning. There was no time to prepare. He was ripped out of my life. And it was my wife, his very own mother, who caused such a brutal separation.

After six months of trauma, (for both Joe and I), and a journey that saw me travel blindly around Thailand in an attempt to find him, father and son were reunited. It was the most traumatic ordeal that I have ever experienced. Yet it taught me a lot about my own character, about the complexity of human nature, about kindness and cruelty, and importantly about the power of love. Lessons that are hard to experience; lessons that I will never forget.

This is my story.

Chapter 1 - The Land of Smiles

I reached up and shoved my bag into the already crammed locker overhead, then settled myself down into the seat next to Dave. I was nervous; it wasn't my first flight, but it was my first flight of such magnitude and my first flight to a place that I knew so little about. I looked at the screen on the back of the headrest in front of me; August the 18th 2005, current location, Birmingham Airport. My final destination, Bangkok Thailand.

An excitement swirled in my gut; I had a feeling about this trip.

"So, what's it like then?" I asked Dave, who was already flicking through the drinks list.

"You'll see when we get there," he smirked, "You've got to get over this flight first."

His failure to quench my thirst for information didn't faze me, and I opened up page one of my Guide to Thailand. Before I had a chance to understand the geography of exactly where I was going the pilot made an announcement, we were preparing for takeoff. I braced myself, feeling the same adrenalin as when I took my first ever flight.

"Here we go mate," Dave said with a grin, and we both looked out as the plane thrust forward and found its position high above the grey gloom that hovered over Birmingham. We were off on the epic flight that would lead to the start of what I hoped would be a magnificent and eye opening holiday. Dave and I amused ourselves with the in flight entertainment, we drank the Thai beer served in the compulsory plastic cup and we slept sporadically to pass the time. My final slumber was interrupted by the chime of the seatbelt warning. I looked around to gauge my bearings, rubbed my eyes and stretched my arms and legs as much as the seating would allow, before preparing myself for landing one of our journey. Dave had only notified me at the last minute that this would be a two part journey, and the landing we were making now was into Dubai airport; we'd been flying for seven hours and we were only halfway there. As we approached the runway I couldn't help but find myself in awe of my surroundings; Dubai looked mystical. Unfortunately we only had a two hour stop here before our next flight and that was to be spent within the confines of the airport. As Dave and I waited I vowed I would return to Dubai one day, and I hoped that as I continued my journey I'd be equally as impressed by my first sight of Bangkok. And within six hours I found out, I stood at the top of the aeroplane steps, motionless. The scale of Bangkok airport alone took my breath away, not to mention the heat that instantly engulfed my body like an uncomfortable film wrapped tightly around me. I marched with purpose towards the impressive airport building; people busied themselves around me rushing from one desk to another, carrying cases and bags that seemed disproportionately big in comparison to the people dragging them across the airport floor. The Tannoy system switched on with a click and a lady's voice filled my ears; the language was musical and combined with her delicately soft tone I was mesmerised. It was presumably a flight announcement but in my ignorance it sounded like the most beautiful poetry or a soothing lullaby.

"Come on mate, this way," Dave nodded his head in the direction of the security desk and a stern looking man sat officiously behind it. I waited in line as one after the other passengers presented themselves and their passports to be scrutinized. It was my turn.

"Stand in front of the desk. Stand on the line," the man barked in English splintered with a twang of Thai.

I wasn't going to question him and I silently followed his instructions.

"Look in the camera," came his next order.

Bloody hell, I thought, they don't mess about here! I had my picture taken, no doubt of me looking bemused and slightly fearful, he snatched my passport and thrust his stamp down onto the centre page. I'd cleared security.

I waited on the other side of the security line for Dave to make an appearance; having been through it all before he took the whole process with an air of cockiness.

"They have to do that," he chuckled, clearly observing my discomfort with the situation, "It's just in case you over stay your welcome."

"Oh right," I replied; they obviously had very strict bureaucracy in this part of the world, I thought.

We walked through to collect our luggage before proceeding without incident to arrivals. Looking out at the sea of taxi drivers beckoning us to their cars I felt a slight panic. Again, confident and seasoned traveller Dave spotted my unease.

"Don't worry mate, I've got it sorted; I've already arranged for a car to pick us up, which means no getting ripped off by any of these drivers," Dave said loudly enough for a few of them to hear as we barged through to the front of the airport.

Before I had a chance to question him he continued, "You have to be careful out here, Sean, everyone's after your money," he spoke with a serious tone that he didn't normally adopt.

"The same as the UK then," I quipped, trying to lighten the mood.

"It's a bit worse than that mate; just be on your toes," he warned before flashing his trademark charmer smile.

He's having me on, I thought, and I pushed his advice to the back of my mind. Outside and looking for our car, the heat was suffocating. I felt as if someone had opened an oven door right in front of my face; I could almost feel my eyebrows being scorched.

"There's our driver." Dave pointed to a bright white car sitting to the right of the airport entrance.

The driver was stood by the bonnet waving frantically with both hands to get our attention; Dave just nodded in acknowledgment and we walked towards him. The driver instantly rushed to take our luggage, beckoning for us to get into the back of the car whilst he loaded up the boot. As I sat down on the cool leather seat I gave thanks for the blast of air conditioning that swept over me like ice cool water. Although I soon realised that my body had already succumbed to the temperature and there was a trail of sweat already trickling down my back and my face was drenched with the same.

With the car loaded up, the driver hurried into the front seat before turning to speak to Dave,

"So, how are you?" he asked.

"Yes, good, although I'll be better once I've had something to eat," Dave replied patting his belly.

The mention of food made my stomach rumble; I'd been so distracted by the sweltering heat that I hadn't noticed the hunger pangs that had been tugging at my insides for the last two hours. I'd never been a fan of aeroplane food, and this flight didn't manage to switch my opinion. I hadn't even been sure what I was eating, it could have been chicken, or lamb, there was even a possibility that it was beef; whatever it was there wasn't enough, and I needed something now, not least to give me the energy to continue my journey; we still had to get to our hotel which was another 30 miles away.

"I better get going then," the driver said starting the car and blasting another surge of icy air into the back. It was heavenly.

Driving through the busy Bangkok streets was like weaving through an obstacle filled maze. Scooters rushed by the car window, at times we were surrounded on all sides by their buzzing motors. Cars drove precariously down pedestrian packed streets and wound round the tower blocks and market stalls without hesitation. There was urgency in the city; everyone had somewhere to be, and their journey seemingly took priority over anyone else's. When we finally left Bangkok the roads became less manic, there was an order that I found comforting; if it wasn't for the unfamiliar road signs and unrecognisable shops that lined the streets, I could've been driving along in a cab in Birmingham. As we drove further out, the buildings that lined the long searching roads gradually disappeared and were replaced with vast expanses of paddy fields.

Every snapshot my eyes took in reminded me of an image in a TV documentary; surreal was an understatement. My fascination with my surroundings grew with each mile we drove. Eventually we entered Pattaya, another busy town with people hurrying about their business on foot, scooters and in cars. And after a short drive we arrived at our hotel; pulling up outside the main entrance I didn't think I could be anymore amazed than I already was. The front of the hotel looked spectacular, the large cream, stone walls, the backdrop to colourful arrangements of tropical plants and flowers. Dave and I eagerly stepped out of the car to be met by a line of smartly dressed staff, all sporting welcoming smiles.

"Sawatdee Kah," they all said in unison, placing their hands together and bowing as they spoke.

I looked nervously over to Dave.

"Just say hello," he urged.

"Hi," I said to one of the petite women standing closest to me.

"Are you from England?" she asked politely.

"Yes."

"We love England," she replied with a smile that was as bright as the sun. "Do you know Beckham?" she asked innocently.

"Oh yes, I used to go to school with him; but he's not as tall in real life as he appears on the TV," I grinned.

"Is that true?" another member of staff questioned.

"Oh yes, he's only a small guy," I bluffed.

The welcome committee, Dave and I burst into spontaneous laughter.

When the hubbub died down Dave explained that I would be shown to my room, and then he suggested that we meet in the bar once we'd both showered and settled in.

"Follow me, sir," a young man spoke softly ahead of me, already laden with my bags. I felt a pang of guilt as I watched him struggle with my hefty luggage, but noticing all the other staff doing the same for the other new arrivals I followed him through the hotel foyer and up to my room. We arrived at my first floor room and the young porter flung open my door, clearly aware of the impression that the scene behind the door would create. I walked in, in a daze; the room was immaculate, with a large bed dominating the main space. I turned to thank the porter but he was already backing away down the corridor, courteously leaving me to enjoy my surroundings. I sat down on the edge of the luxurious bed. Two plane flights, one car and almost 24 hours travelling and I'd made it; my holiday in Thailand could begin.

Chapter 2 – Kim

I dumped my bags in the corner of the room and headed straight for the bathroom; the pressing heat had taken its toll and I was yearning for a cool shower to wash away the stress and the unforgiving sweat, and to reinvigorate my tired body. I made my way into the spacious bathroom, peeled off my travelling clothes and stepped into the shower cubicle. I turned the tap and let the large shower head work its magic, pounding down a continuous blast of refreshment. I let some of the water trickle into my mouth as I washed, although I wasn't entirely sure if it was safe to drink. If only I'd actually read my guide books, I thought to myself with a chuckle, spitting out another mouthful, just in case.

With my shower reluctantly over, I pulled out a crisp white shirt and some light cream trousers from my case. They could've done with an iron, but with the call of a nice cool beer echoing in the distance I opted against it and quickly got dressed and headed down to the bar, where I'd agreed to meet Dave. Walking into the bar area I was greeted by a sea of smiling faces, all nodding their heads politely in my direction. I smiled back, I couldn't help it; it was infectious. I ordered my first beer of the holiday and perched on the bar stool whilst it was poured, preparing to savour the first sip. The glass was placed on a small white coaster in front of me; I spotted the delicate hand first and then, as I looked up I saw her smile; a smile that shone brighter than any I'd ever seen.

"Thank you," I managed, trying not to stare at the beauty that had served me my drink.

She flicked her long black hair over her shoulder, revealing another coy and captivating smile as she did so.

"I'm Sean," I said, not that she'd asked, but I felt compelled to speak to her, to find out more.

"I'm Kim," she replied, "Where are you from, Sean?"

I'd never heard my name pronounced as delicately as she'd just said it, I grinned, "I'm from England."

"I love England, I go to school to learn English; everybody speaks English all round the world, that means England is number one." Her words tripped over one another as they gushed from her mouth, but I hung from every single syllable. I'd never considered the fact that we could be viewed as number one, as she'd so innocently put it, and before I had the chance to think about it any further, she spoke again.

"I like your tattoos," she said, pointing to the colourful ink that adorned my forearm, in stark contrast to the bright white of my short sleeved shirt.

"Thank you," I replied, feeling slightly self conscious as the victim of her enchanting stare. "Do you have any?"

"No! My mum would run after me with a knife if I had one," she squealed. I burst into laughter at the thought.

"I see you're making yourself at home then," a voice came from behind me.

I turned round to see a freshly showered Dave, wearing the first of his 'holiday shirts' and some long tailored shorts. He gave me a sly look in reference to the beautiful Kim who was still standing angelically behind the bar. I acknowledged him with a tight lipped smirk.

"Come on mate, let's eat, I'm starving," Dave said, tugging my arm to pull me away from the bar. I needed that pull; if it was left to me I would've stayed and chatted to Kim all night.

We made our way over to the nearest free table and each sat down either side, only separated by the pressed white linen tablecloth which was topped with a single tropical flower in a tiny glass vase.

A waitress handed me a leather bound menu, I opened it apprehensively, convinced I'd have no idea what anything was. Dave sensed my uncertainty.

"Its ok mate, the menu's in Thai and English,"

"Thank goodness for that," I said sweeping the back of my hand across my forehead in exaggerated relief.

I took another swig of my beer before trawling through the menu occasionally reading out some of the more extravagant dishes that caught my eye. It all looked so good, combinations of meat, sauces and vegetables that I'd never even considered and yet every single one looked appealing. But I decided to play it safe on the first night, and opted for an old favourite.

"I'll have the steak and chips please," I said to the waitress as I handed the menu back. She nodded politely but clearly amused by my lack of adventure, "And two more beers please," I added as I drained the last drops from my glass.

"This is the life," Dave said as he sat back in his chair and surveyed the peaceful surroundings. The only movement came from the staff rushing almost silently about their business, tending to the few diners sat embracing the holiday atmosphere.

Within moments a waiter came to the table and presented our beers, served in a case to keep them cool in the still overpowering heat of the evening. I glanced over at the bar and spotted Kim, my eyes were drawn to her, following her every move as she walked from one end to the other, every now and then stopping to chat with her face glowing with kindness and sincerity as she spoke. She saw me looking; I shot my eyes back to

13

the tablecloth, but for some reason I looked back, and there it was, that smile, her full lips turned up at the corners and parted just enough to show her perfect white teeth. She was truly mesmerising.

Our meals were eventually served and Dave and I got stuck in, the lengthy journey had drained us both and we needed the hearty feast to revive us. We made small talk as we ate, I ribbed Dave about his shirt, and he ribbed me about my obviously creased attire but all the while I felt as though I was being watched. I felt Kim's gem like eyes following my every mouthful, every hand gesture, every word. I'd almost finished the juicy steak when she approached the table;

"How is your meal, Sean," she said, seemingly not interested in Dave's opinion.

"It's beautiful," I replied, dabbing my mouth with my napkin to make sure there were no telltale signs of the rate I'd been shovelling it down.

"Yes, we like to cook."

"It shows," I replied with honesty.

We spoke for some time, my remaining chips went cold but I wasn't concerned, I was enjoying myself. The conversation flowed, despite her slightly broken English, which I found endearing, and we both seemed fascinated by the other.

I spotted one of Kim's colleagues trying to catch her attention, "I think you're wanted," I said, nodding towards the other woman looking in need of help at the end of the bar.

"Ah yes, I shall speak with you later, Sean," Kim said rushing to help her friend. I sat back and watched as the dainty woman moved away, but my thoughts were soon interrupted by a raucous laughter from the other side of the table.

"We've only just got here and you're at it already!" Dave said, still chuckling to himself.

I didn't reply; I didn't feel like I was 'at it'; I wasn't sure what I was doing, I just knew that she was the prettiest women I'd ever seen, and the culmination of her beauty was embodied in her hypnotic smile. We left our table and moved back to the bar for some more drinks and it wasn't long before Kim and I found ourselves talking again.

"Do you want me to show you round?" she offered, "its fine, work won't mind, I'm about to finish soon anyway," she reassured.

I couldn't think of any good reason to say no and yet there were millions of reasons to say yes.

"I'll take you to the beach."

What the hell, I thought, keen to throw myself in at the deep end.

"Some mate you are," Dave joked, "I was going to show you about, but I guess I won't bother now."

"I'll see you later," I laughed in response. Dave knew a lot of people where we were, so I knew he'd easily be able to amuse himself, no doubt frequent a few bars and meet up with some old friends.

Before I had time to apologise to him Kim scooped my hand up in hers and led me out of the main door. The night had drawn in, the moon was low in the charcoal sky but the temperature was still on par with a midday heat.

"It's so warm," I said conscious of my hand becoming moist in her affectionate grip.

"Oh yes, very, very hot, that's why my skin is black and you look like milk," she giggled.

I loved her analogies.

We walked out onto the main street, the roads were still bustling, cars and scooters weaved in and out of each other, the sea of brake lights frantically flashing on and off. Ordinarily I would have felt uneasy with the crowds but feeling Kim's gentle squeeze on my hand as she led me through the streets, calmed my nerves and filled me with peace.

"Come, come," she said excitedly, as she picked up her step to a slight jog. And in seconds I could see why she was so excited. In front of me stretched a long and tranquil beach, bright lights dotted along its length like runway lights, allowing us to appreciate the fine sand that rolled out into the dark sea. I froze; it was paradise. Another gentle squeeze encouraged me to walk down onto the warm sand.

We walked and we talked; each taking our turn to fire questions and soak up the other's intriguing answers. I spoke of my life in England and she spoke about her very different life in Thailand, her family, their farm.

"A farm?" I questioned, "Wow, I take it your family is quite wealthy then?"

This time it was Kim laughing at my naivety.

"You are funny," she said, "No, everyone has a farm here, we grow coffee, but we're certainly not rich."

"Oh," I said slightly embarrassed at my ignorance.

"That's why I work at the hotel; I send my money back to my family, because I love them very much."

The matter of fact nature of her statement choked me. A kindness that came so organically from her soul and expressed in a way that I knew would rarely be seen in the UK.

I was speechless. We walked some more in a comfortable silence before finding a spot on the beach to sit down together. I put my arm around the delicate woman sat next to me and found her snuggling her head into my chest, I stroked her glossy hair with my hand before gently placing my lips on the top of her head. She looked up and stared straight at me before responding with a warm kiss. The evening became a blur of kissing, talking, laughing and learning; learning about each other and about the instinctive something that connected us. And it was all played out in front of the lapping sea, with the stars as our audience.

Chapter 3 – Enlightenment

It was the early hours of the morning before we started to head back to the hotel; the night had rushed past us without us even noticing, we'd been captivated by each other, there was no need for an awareness of time, there was no space in my mind for consideration of such inconsequential matters; all I could think about was the beautiful woman I'd spent the night with. We'd hit it off big time, this was something powerful.

Back in my hotel room daybreak burst through the bedroom window and woke me from my doze, as I struggled to accept the brilliant sunrays into my tired eyes I noticed my situation. Kim was still sleeping silently, her dark hair strewn across my arm as she nuzzled into my chest. I couldn't help but smile. She must have sensed my attention as within seconds she too was slowly opening her eyes; she looked up at me with a shy grin. She had a delicate vulnerability in her tired state. I kissed her good morning, brimming with a buzz I hadn't felt for a long time, if ever.

We both showered and dressed, I opted for a pale blue t-shirt and some long grey shorts, Kim put on her tightly fitting uniform that she'd worn the night before. As she stood in front of the mirror combing her fingers through her ruffled hair, I couldn't help but pan my eyes across her perfect frame. She caught me looking but it didn't faze her, she just carried on making herself look even more beautiful, although at that exact moment I didn't think it was possible. We slowly made our way downstairs for breakfast; we sat at the same table Dave and I had eaten at the night before, I laughed to myself as I mused how much I preferred the sight of this morning's guest over last night's dinner 'date'. Some of Kim's colleagues came over to our

18

table, the group of four girls excitedly babbled, with high pitch squeals audible amongst the impressive flow of their fluent tongue. I sat quietly observing the girlish giggles that were being targeted in my direction.

"I hope this is all good," I said, not entirely sure what to make of the whispers, squeaks and darted looks.

"What do you do as a job, Sean?" the tallest girl of the bunch said coyly.

"Oh I'm a doctor," I said, I couldn't help but initiate a wind up. Kim looked at me with a muted smirk; she knew I was playing with them, she'd heard almost everything about me last night on the beach; she knew I was only a builder.

"A Doctor?" the girl questioned, wide eyed.

"Yes, you can call me Doctor Seany if you want?" I tried my hardest not to let my face crack and give the game away.

"Okay Doctor Seany," she said, turning to walk back to the other girls who had been called back to the bar to start their shift. I watched her as she met them, and chuckled at the others' reactions, clearly impressed if not a little shocked to find out about my medical prowess!

"A doctor?" Kim looked at me with mock disapproval, "You are a bad man Doctor Seany."

We both laughed, the outburst resounding amid the tangible chemistry between us.

We ordered breakfast, both opting for what we knew best and after a short time my American breakfast was presented to me, laden high with eggs and ham it looked a mammoth meal compared to Kim's delicate portion of tropical fruit and her small porcelain bowl filled with rice and chicken. It looked lovely, but it didn't seem like a proper breakfast to me. We both tucked in, the long night had certainly made us hungry, and for a few minutes we sat in silence, concentrating on restoring some energy to our weary bodies. Then the silence was broken.

"Have you ever been to a temple?" Kim's question seemed to explode from the thoughts in her mind.

"Err, no, never. I've been to churches but never a temple," I replied, trying to work out when I would have visited such a place.

"Churches, is that Jesus Christ?"

"Well I haven't seen him yet and don't want to for a long time," I said.

"Why is he not a nice person?" Her innocence amused me.

"No, he's a very nice person," I replied, "But it's just not my time to talk to him," I smiled. I could tell this particular piece of humour was completely lost on my breakfast companion and I struggled not to laugh out loud, at my joke or at the comedy being lost in translation.

"Well, I think I'll take you, to a temple, not to Jesus," Kim said still looking confused.

"That'd be great." In all honesty I didn't care where we went as long as I got to spend more time with her.

We carried on eating, I finished every last morsel on my plate, slumping back in my chair and rubbing my bloated belly on completion. It was just what Doctor Seany had ordered, well almost, I'd have preferred a full English; who uses ham instead of bacon, I thought to myself looking down at a tiny scrap of meat I'd missed. It had done the job though and that was all that mattered, and I imagined that by the end of the holiday I'd be well and truly converted to the American way of doing things, well breakfast at least.

We stood up from the table in unison and I pressed the palms of my hands together before saying, 'thank you' in Thai, to the waitresses standing to one side. I surprised myself that I'd mastered my first phrase already.

"Bye Doctor Seany," came a singsong chorus from the girls.

I replied with a smile and then Kim took my hand and led me out of the hotel and on to the main street that led away and into the main town. I felt excited, nervous, and bursting with adrenalin, despite my breakfast urging me to slow down in order to digest it. Kim was excited too, she practically skipped down the street, with me in tow. Then she flung out her delicate arm with a certainty that would've made any vehicle grind to a halt not just the taxi that she was now ushering me into.

We sat together in the back of the cab, luckily it was another air conditioned car as I wasn't quite ready to suffer at the mercy of the heat yet; it was only 10 am after all. Kim led the conversation for most of the journey, at times I felt my mind wandering from her words as I focused instead on the vision that sat next to me, oozing with affection and with dark eyes that swallowed me up every time I allowed myself to look into them for too long. The journey was only a short one, and the chaos of the main road soon became a tranquil stillness as we approached the temple. We pulled up at the entrance, even the taxi's previously squeaking brakes seemed to respect the importance of the building and chose to function in silence on our arrival. I pulled out some money from my wallet, I still hadn't gotten to grips with the currency so Kim helped me sort out exactly how much to hand to the driver, then we shuffled out of the door to find ourselves stood at the temple entrance. I was dumbstruck. Directly in front of me were two huge, ornately decorated dragons, with wisps of brilliant golds and lustrous reds bringing a lifelike reality to the statues. The dragons flanked a large stone staircase that led up a steep hill towards the temple entrance, the centre of each step clearly worn by the number of worshippers and visitors that had made the journey to the top. Bloody hell, I thought to myself, as a flashback from one of my favourite childhood TV programmes came to my mind, this is like monkey magic. I looked over to Kim, who was once again gripping my left hand. I decided not to share my revelation; that would've been a translation too far.

"Shall we?" she said, opening out a hand towards the first step.

I didn't need to be asked twice, if the entrance was that impressive I couldn't wait to see the interior. We started with a good pace but the burning sun, complete lack of shade and the tortuous gradient of the steps, meant I couldn't keep up the healthy stride I'd started with. By the time we reached the summit I'd almost given up trying to placate the constant pool of sweat that soaked my brow and dripped rather obviously off the tip of my nose. With one last sweep of my forehead across the sleeve of my t-shirt I turned around and look down. I opened my mouth but I couldn't even think of the words to use let alone voice them.

"Wow," I said dreamily, slightly disappointed that that was all I could muster when faced with such magnificence. This was the first time I'd seen Thailand properly, although looking out it seemed like I'd seen it before, in a dream perhaps, of paradise lost. Pattaya looked enormous as I stretched my line of sight out to the coast line.

"This is amazing," I said, mopping my brow once more to stop the sweat that was threatening to drip down and blur my vision.

Kim flashed her bright smile at me once more, "Come, come," she said, tugging gently at my hand to pull me towards some more giant statues; again the extravagant décor left me speechless, colours so bold and golds and bronzes that shimmered so brightly in the sunlight, it made it difficult to look at the extravagant sculptures for too long. As we approached them Kim bent down and picked up some incense sticks, without a word she lit them and then walked a few paces before crouching down and then slowly repositioning herself onto her knees. She clasped her hands together, her eyes followed suit, and she began to speak. I wasn't quite sure of my place in the proceedings, I awkwardly looked around, the calmness that I'd felt when we arrived was multiplied tenfold now we were inside. There were lots of people, all carrying out their own ritualistic acts, but all I could really see was Kim. I watched as she squeezed her eyes tighter together, a slight frown appearing in her forehead as she did so and I watched her mouth seemingly moving with more passion, more determination. It was a beautiful moment, spiritually, emotionally and physically. A sight I knew then that I would never forget. After a short while she opened her eyes, composed herself and then slowly stood up and walked towards me. She reached up and pressed her lips on mine, the strength of her kiss seemingly trying to tell me something.

"Thank you," I said, not sure if that was the right response or not.

"You're welcome, Sean," her soft voice tinged with intensity.

"What were you praying for, if you don't mind me asking?" I said, again not sure if that was an appropriate request or not.

She looked into my eyes with a force that compelled me to look back with just as much passion.

"I was asking if I could spend my life with you, and be happy. I want my life to be happy."

Her stare had not wavered. She means this, I thought. Then from nowhere came another thought; I want your life to be happy too.

Chapter 4 – The Two Headed Dragon

Hand in hand we walked down the large concrete staircase, away from the temple where I'd only moments before felt that breathtaking realisation. The journey down was by far a preferable trek to the journey up; I breezed down the worn cascade of steps, the warm buzz in my stomach somehow contributing to my almost childlike bound downwards.

"Come with me," Kim urged when we reached the bottom, the spring in her step reflecting my own.

"I'll take you on a tuk tuk," she said looking out across the road in front of us.

I wasn't quite sure what to expect as she shouted something to a small guy resting astride a motorbike. His initial disposition of indifference was swiftly replaced with an unnatural keenness, and before I had a chance to question what the fascinating trail of words she'd just voiced actually meant, the man and his motorbike, complete with what looked like a bus seat attached precariously on the back, were positioned eagerly in front of us.

"You don't expect me to fit in there do you?" my eyes bulged with a nervous uncertainty. Kim just giggled her girly giggle.

"Come on Sean, you'll be ok, trust me," she beamed.

I must be off my head I thought, as I climbed up on to the tatty seat, sitting down to cover the flash of yellow foam that burst out of the ripped, burnt red, leather cushion. This was another new experience that I'm sure even the greatest guide book couldn't have prepared me for. Before we had even joined the main stream of traffic I'd begun to question whether the driver even had a licence. This guy is bloody crazy, I thought as I watched his head weave from side to side as if he was leaning into the bends at the TT races. In and out of the traffic our bike and bus seat darted, I was on a rollercoaster ride through the streets of Thailand, and Kim and the ride operator seemingly found my white knuckle experience hilarious.

"Oh my god, don't take me now, please!" I yelled in jest; remnants of real fear echoing in the background.

The driver turned his head back, laughing at his novice passenger's reaction.

"Keep your eyes on the road, for god sake!" I blasted.

By the time we reached our destination I felt like I'd manoeuvred my way through a computer game, pedestrians and other equally crazy drivers being the obstacles and the enemies I had to avoid to complete the level. I couldn't quite decide who'd won as I got down from the seat, my legs shaking beneath me.

"You're so funny Sean," Kim placed her hand tenderly on my arm as she spoke.

"I'm glad you think it's funny," I said smiling. I thought for a moment about how natural the chemistry between us was; natural and growing with every breath.

"We'll have something to eat and drink," Kim said pointing for me to enter the café that we'd pulled up outside. "Then we can go to the beach again."

Kim's plan was as perfect as any I could come up with.

"Sounds good," I replied, thankful to be able to rest my still wobbling legs as I sat down on one of the white plastic seats that were crammed together outside the café. I turned my head to locate the source of the welcome breeze; a giant fan was whirring gently behind me, drying the moisture seeping into my collar.

Kim ordered drinks for the both of us; it intrigued me how she could switch from English to Thai so effortlessly. I felt the need to make more of an effort to embrace her culture.

"What's Thai food like, Kim?" I asked, my eyes searching the menu for something vaguely familiar.

"It's very nice; have you not tried it?" Kim replied, clearly shocked at my lack of adventure.

"No... I like curry, as long as it's not too hot," I said cautiously. The heat was already blistering, so the thought of a mouth full of fiery spices on top of that, certainly didn't sound appetising. But I wanted to eat something Thai; I wanted to show Kim the respect that she'd shown for me and all things English.

Once again she ordered in her mother tongue, assuring me afterwards that the chicken dish to come would be a mild one, and most definitely wouldn't leave me scrambling for jugs of water.

As Kim continued chatting to the waitress I gazed around; on the opposite side of the road I noticed some scaffolders, a familiar sight from back home I thought to myself, but as I looked harder I realised a very real difference between the Thai scaffolders and the English ones. In Thailand the scaffold poles were made from Bamboo, and they were lashed together with rope; I was astonished. I watched as the barefooted workmen leaped from level to level, like children tackling a climbing frame. How different things are here I chuckled, UK health and safety would have a field day over here I thought, before my mind came back to our side of the road and the beautiful young woman sat staring affectionately at me from the other side of the table.

Before I could explain why I was so astounded our food was placed down on the small circular table for two.

I looked on with trepidation, "Oh well, here goes," I said as I compiled the first fork full of rice and chicken; making sure to go heavy on the rice, just in case Kim's idea of mild didn't exactly concur with mine. The flavour hit the front of my tongue as I popped it in my mouth and then I felt the devil himself reach in, put his hand down my throat and squeeze my insides. My eyes were watering, my mouth didn't know whether to open or shut. I gulped down the entire fork of fire.

"Shit, shit, shit." I waved my right hand frantically in front of my face as I spoke. I started to blow out short sharp gusts of air; it wasn't helping. I tried reversing the action and sucking in channels of air in an attempt to cool my burning tongue. Nothing was helping. And then in my panic and through my streaming eyes I realised Kim was almost crying with laughter.

"You meant that didn't you, you did that on purpose," I said, her mischievous streak endearing me to her even more.

She could barely speak for laughing, every time she opened her mouth she just chuckled again.

I just smiled as I guzzled down the ice cold coke in front of me.

"I'll get you back," I laughed, "You just wait and see."

"But you're a doctor, Sean, you should be able to make yourself better," Kim managed to say once she'd finally controlled her laughter. That just set me off again, and so there we were, the two of us laughing at nothing and everything.

The laughter subsided and we continued the meal, although I had no choice but to only indulge in the rice. Once we'd had our fill Kim reached across the table and held my hand, then leant over to offer me another tender kiss.

"Let's go back to the hotel," she announced.

"Sounds good to me," I replied. I couldn't believe that this day, this moment, was happening to me.

*****

We showered at the hotel and then walked down towards the beach; it was the first time I'd seen it in the daylight; the sea was picture perfect as it lapped on the sand that seemed to spread for miles like a covering of golden silk along the coastline.

As always Kim knew exactly where my next adventure would take me and I excitedly jumped into the waiting speedboat that Kim had arranged to take us across to one of the islands. We flew through the calm sea, the spray from the back of the boat whipping up ferociously behind us, the noise as we cut through the air making it impossible for us to engage in conversation, so we just sat, for twenty minutes, looking at one another, and grinning.

I stepped out of the boat onto the sands of an island that looked even more beautiful than the Pattaya beach we'd just left. We agreed on a spot to lay down our towels and we stretched our bodies out on top of them. We lay there for hours, talking, laughing, and both surprised at how unquestionably at ease we were in each other's company. There was a charming language barrier that at times brought a look of confusion on one or both of our faces, but even that couldn't initiate any awkwardness between us. It was as if I was lying on the beach with a lifelong friend.

The sun started to fall from its parapet and reluctantly we knew it was time to head back. It had been a long but amazing day, and Kim felt it too. So much so that she wasn't prepared to end it there.

"I've been talking to one of my friends," she said as she stepped out of the hotel shower. "She's told me of a good club, I will take you, ok?"

"Yes, that sounds great." I would've said yes to anything she'd suggested if it meant spending more time with her; I might've even attempted another curry, I thought to myself as I reminisced fondly about the day.

We both got ready to go out, a white shirt with a faint cheque pattern, teamed with some light trousers and some tan shoes, was my outfit of choice. Kim put on a scarlet red dress that she'd grabbed from her locker on the way up to my room. I watched in awe as she brushed her jet black locks in an almost regal fashion. Then when we were both ready I proudly walked with her hand in mine, as we made our way to the club. The club was an outdoor venue, which meant I could benefit from the cool breeze that sauntered past the clubbers as the night set in. Most of the partygoers were couples, enjoying the music, drinking and making the most of the Thai nightlife. Kim and I danced like our lives depended on it; moving together in an almost rehearsed harmony. Between dancing bouts, Kim sat on my lap, laughing with me, chatting about our similarities and finding out more about our fascinating differences. It was a perfect evening that ended in a perfect way, with Kim wrapped in my arms in my hotel room.

The next morning we woke up in a leisurely fashion and made our way downstairs for breakfast. "Morning doctor Seany," came the chorus from the courteous welcoming committee; each with their palms pushed firmly together.

I copied their action, "Good morning," I sang back.

At that moment in time I couldn't have felt anymore satisfied with life, the reality of life back in England was a distant and fading memory. This magical place was starting to feel like a home that I didn't ever want to leave.

Kim and I sat down to take breakfast and as I perused the menu a voice interrupted my paradise tranquillity.

"Where the bloody hell have you been?" I could tell Dave's question wasn't actually searching for a factual answer, so I decided against giving him the full rundown of the temple and the deserted island.

"I've been busy mate."

"I can see that," he said smirking at Kim. He pulled out one of the free chairs around our table for four, and sat down.

"You look like you had a good night," I said, noticing the unmistakable hangover frown.

"I can't complain," he said with a wink. "So, you in love then?" He continued.

"I'm having a great time, Dave," I said, not wanting to get drawn in to his shameful attempts to embarrass me.

"I can see that!" he replied.

I could see in his eyes he thought I was a bloody fool to be spending all my time with Kim, but I didn't want to stay in the bars all day and night; I'd come on the holiday of a lifetime and I was enjoying it the way I wanted to.

"So what you up to today then," Dave continued, a tone of mockery in his voice.

"I don't know mate," I replied, looking over to Kim for our itinerary for the day.

"I will take you to the market?" Came her words on cue.

"Yeah, ok then," I nodded.

"You looking for a wedding ring then?" Dave couldn't help himself.

"I don't think so," I squirmed jokingly. All three of us started to laugh.

"So, what you up to, Dave?"

"I don't know yet, I've got to meet up with a couple of lads in the Diana bar later."

I rolled my eyes; surely he can see there's more to Thailand than just getting drunk in the bars twenty four hours a day, I thought to myself.

The conversation ended abruptly as we tucked into the mounds of breakfast that streamed onto the table; fruit platters, breads, eggs, the supply of treats didn't seem to stop; which was handy as I assumed a day at the market would require a lot of stamina, and I wasn't entirely sure that I'd be able to find something Sean friendly for lunch either.

"Come on then, I'll show you the market," Kim said standing up from her chair the second I'd finished my last mouthful.

I loved her enthusiasm for life.

"Ok," I said, taking her lead and standing up from my chair, "I'll see you later, Dave."

"And you will," he said smiling, "Have a good one!"

"I will," I grinned unable to hide my excitement from Dave's judgemental shaking head and pursed mouth.

Outside the hotel the heat hit me like a punch from Bruno.

"I still can't get over how hot it is here," I said to Kim, dropping her hand from mine to find a hanky to mop my brow.

"You baby, Sean," she said laughing in a way that reached in and inflated my heart.

As we walked through the busy streets I found myself engulfed in a cloud of aromas; car fumes, mixed with warm spices and hot bodies all intensified in a bubble of searing humidity. People were rushing around, opening shops, meeting each other, passing each other and going about their business, all of them with unfailing smiles. As I watched the rest of Pattaya getting ready to start work, it dawned on me that Kim had not worked since the night we met.

"Do the hotel not mind you spending all your time with me?" I asked, concerned that she was risking her job for me.

"No, they're all happy that I've met you. I was on my own, Sean. I have nobody."

I felt for her, and my face obviously showed it, as she clarified her comment.

"I have lots of friends, Sean, but no boyfriend."

"Will you still get paid?"

"No, but I don't mind, I'm having a holiday with you. When you go home I'm going back to stay with my mum on the farm."

"Oh right," I said, a little confused by the whole conversation.

"What will you be doing there?"

She laughed at me, "Working Sean, working very hard."

I sighed, "Yes, and me," I said trying desperately not to think about real life.

And as we walked and talked we finally entered the hustle of the market.

"This isn't like any market I've ever seen," I said, bemused by the sights around me.

Fish lay lined up for inspection on the vendors tables; dogs sat forlorn in cages; birds screeched their desperate cries from behind their bars. I tried to think of something that you just wouldn't expect to find at a market, but within seconds I found it.

"This is unreal," I said to Kim, trying to work out exactly what meat the burly man was trying to sell me.

"You can buy very, very cheap clothes here, Sean," Kim said pulling me away from the table of carcasses.

"Oh right, ok."

We walked over to the clothes stall, they were ridiculously cheap, and I felt rude paying so little for my new shirts and shorts, and the dress that I treated Kim to. But not wanting to insult them I duly paid and walked away.

"I'd like to spend the rest of the day in the pool," Kim announced once we'd browsed the majority of the market.

I was more than happy with her suggestion; a chance to cool off for more than five minutes in an air conditioned doorway. The hotel had a pool on the roof; we made our way up there to be met by Dave who was accompanied by an attractive Thai girl with a short black bob and wearing a lime green bikini.

"Bloody hell, twice in one day, you feeling all right?" He jested.

"Yes mate, I see you've found a new friend then, Dave," I said in an attempt to reverse the ribbing.

"Oh yeah, I was lonely."

"Yeah, right," I scoffed.

We spent most of the day in the pool, Kim splashed about as best she could, she was a weak swimmer to say the least, but to be honest I wasn't really paying much attention to her swimming prowess. All I could see was that she looked like something out of a Bond film; her hot pink swimsuit showed off every perfect curve in her body. I couldn't take my eyes off her. How was I lucky enough to find a woman like this, I thought to myself as she tried her hardest to splash me as I lounged by the side of the pool.

That night Kim and I didn't leave our hotel room; we made the most of room service, ordering food and drinks late into the night. We lay entwined on the bed, watching TV together like an old married couple. I couldn't comprehend the language but I got the gist of the story, and as I lay there laughing at a dodgy comedy sketch, that I didn't quite understand, one word came to mind; blissful.

Chapter 5 – Back to the smoke

The two weeks I spent in Thailand flew by, dotted with further demonstrations of blissfulness. I had just one day left before I had to board the plane back to my mundane life in dreary old England. I tried my hardest not to dwell on the end, needing to make the most of every last second with Kim. And we chose to spend our final full day together on our paradise beach; inevitably we found ourselves talking about what would happen when our bubble was popped, when I left for the first leg of my journey to Bangkok.

"I don't want to think about it Kim," I said, "Back to the grindstone and all that."

Kim looked blankly at me; although her English was good, she hadn't managed to get to grips with some of our quirkier sayings.

"Never mind," I laughed, "I'm just not looking forward to going back to work, the stress of being the boss, it's hard." I paused. "But the stress of walking away from you is going to be harder."

I felt like my heart was being ripped out just at the thought of leaving her. Kim's mournful face told me she felt the same. There was no doubt we'd fallen in love. And at that moment I cursed the fact that I had. Two souls so perfectly connected and yet from such different worlds and so far apart that the cruel reality was, the only option was to be thankful that we'd met and accept that we never would again.

"I can come back to Bangkok with you," Kim suddenly shrieked, breaking the wake-like stillness.

"What do you mean?"

"I've a friend in Bangkok; I can travel with you, stay there before I go to mother's farm."

Her excitement meant her sentence was interspersed with Thai but I could still understand.

"That's a great idea!"

We kissed a long kiss, savouring the fact that we'd found a way to delay the inevitable for a few hours at least, and for now we could get back to enjoying our time together.

After our last night in the hotel together Kim and I walked down to the reception desk to settle my final bill. Dave had already checked out and was waiting outside talking to the driver. As I made my way out to join him the hotel manager walked across the hotel foyer.

"You're welcome at my hotel any time," he said with a sincere Thai smile. "If you come back to Thailand you stay at my hotel, ok?"

"Yes I will, thank you," I replied, silently praying to anyone that would listen, to get me back there sooner rather than later.

And just as they had done when I arrived the staff lined up at the hotel entrance to say their goodbyes, all with their hands pressed together in the traditional way. I'd never felt so emotional about a holiday coming to an end, but then again I'd never been to Thailand before.

I handed my luggage to the driver to load into the car.

"Bye doctor Seany," the line of women shouted harmoniously from behind me.

I turned around and smiled. It was a very sad day.

Dave, Kim and I settled into the car for the journey back to Bangkok. Dave sat up front while Kim and I sat in silence in the back, a gentle squeeze of our clasped hands the only communication we needed to express how devastated we were both feeling.

The journey that had seemed to take so long on the way to Pattaya, now seemed like a quick trip to the next street, and solemnly the car soon pulled up outside Bangkok airport. I gulped down a ball of emotion, took a deep breath and opened the car door. I couldn't bring myself to look at Kim.

We loaded our luggage onto a trolley that Dave had commandeered; he said his goodbyes to Kim and walked ahead through the large glass doors.

I turned to the melancholy beauty that I held in my arms, "I'll call you when I get back home."

"Promise?"

"Yes, of course, you know me, Kim. I'm a man of my word." And even if I wasn't I was sure she could see the sincerity in my eyes.

I knew it was coming to an end and I knew I had to deal with it swiftly. I leant forward and left her with a kiss that I hoped told her I'd be back. I dragged my body through the glass doors, fighting the inner urge to turn and run back towards her. I took one last look back.

I'd never really understood the term *gutted*, but there and then, the hollow ache in my belly forced me to acknowledge that that was exactly what I was.

In the departure lounge I flicked through my camera, in awe of the images, a collection of the most amazing experiences and memories I'd ever known, and within almost every picture was a vision of the most beautiful woman I'd ever seen.

"Bloody hell, you've got it bad," Dave sneered, cutting me short from showing him yet another photo.

"I've just had the greatest holiday of my life, that's all," I protested.

"Well back to reality now, it's over." I didn't appreciate Dave's blunt tone, and I turned away from his disapproving look. Just as I did so an announcement came over the Tannoy system. I froze, and listened carefully as it was repeated; our flight had been cancelled. I looked across at Dave, his face was screwed up with annoyance, but I couldn't help but burst into spontaneous laughter.

"Does that mean we can stay then?" I questioned through my chuckles, already picturing running out of the airport to find Kim.

"Let's go and find out what the hell's going on," Dave said with a tut and a heavy sigh.

We joined the queue at the Emirates desk, and after ten minutes of confusion and some skilful dodging of the irate arms of some Thai businessmen, we were advised that we would be put up in a hotel for the night, and would be flying home the following day.

Dave and I were shown to our room, it wasn't exactly majestic but it was comfortable enough for the night. The two single beds were separated by a small wooden cabinet.

"I hope you don't bloody snore, Dave," I said as I sat down on the bed nearest the window.

"I was thinking the same about you, Sean," as he lay back on the free bed. He reached his hands up to rest them behind his head, then turned to look at the bedside cabinet that separated us.

"Look they've even left you a present," he said as he pointed to the box of Durex that sat awkwardly on top of the cabinet.

I laughed, "Yes, and they better still be there in the morning, no funny business, I'm a deep sleeper."

"Come on you joker," Dave said springing back up to his feet, "Let's go down to the bar and grab a beer."

I didn't need to be asked twice; the bar was busy, with families, couples and lone travellers all trying to make the most of being stranded. We sat down with our drinks and I pulled out my phone.

"Who you calling?" Dave asked.

I looked up and gave him a look that suggested he didn't need to ask. I was texting Kim. And as if she was waiting for my message her text came back almost instantly. She was coming to meet us.

The last chance evening came and went, and before I knew it we were back at the airport having another heart wrenching re-enactment of the goodbyes we'd rehearsed the day before. But this time there was no last minute reprieve, I got on the plane; I was on my way back to the UK.

*****

I stepped out of the taxi, the clouds laid heavy over Cannock; I rummaged in my pocket to find some cash to pay the driver. Struggling to separate the Sterling from the Baht I got caught in the welcome home downpour. I handed over the cash, heaved my bag out of the boot and vaulted over a puddle towards my front door. I turned the key in the lock before trudging through a pile of junk mail and bills. I dumped my bag in the hallway and looked around at my cold, lifeless home.

I knew coming back from a holiday always instigated a comedown but this felt so much more intense. I walked through to the front room and slumped into the sofa; I wanted to be back in Thailand so badly, and almost subconsciously I found myself once again flicking through my photographic memories. At the same time I remembered my phone was still switched off from the flight, I reached into my jean pocket, pulled out my phone, turned it on, flung it on the sofa, and continued reminiscing. It wasn't long before the beeps started, the beeps that signalled the start of a stream of text messages from Kim.

As I read through them I realised she was missing me as much as I was missing her, and it had only been a day. Without thinking my fingers dialled her number.

"Kim, it's me. Are you ok?"

"I'm missing you, Sean," came the delayed reply, "I didn't want you to go home."

"Well I'll come and see you again; I promised didn't I?"

I tried to reassure her but I had no idea when or how I would get back there.

And as I climbed into my empty bed that evening I still hadn't worked it out. The next day I tried to get back into the old work routine; the drive up to the office was as tedious as it ever had been. The queries and hassles that I'd left behind were all still there, all with the same pressing importance, and yet I couldn't or wouldn't take it all in. My sunburnt skin reminded me every second of where I'd just been; the bitter cold air reminded me what I was missing, and the pain in my chest reminded me that Kim was almost as far away from me as she could possibly be. I couldn't get her out of my head. I glided through the day in a haze until six o clock saw me sitting back in my empty flat feeling numb. And the cycle continued over the weeks that followed; I went through the motions of living my pre Thailand life, but the only time I actually felt like I was living was when I spoke to Kim, which I did every night, those phone calls were my raison d'être.

It was a grey Wednesday morning when I made the decision to search for a cheap flight back; I'd pulled my curtains open that morning and was almost compelled to shut them again when I saw the dank sky and miserable faces walking past. Within half an hour I'd logged on to my computer and booked the flight to Bangkok. I felt a wave of relief calm the tension from my body. I needed to know why I was feeling so low, I needed to know if there was something real between Kim and I, or whether I simply had the most intense post holiday blues known to man.

In work the next day I started chatting to Mark, the Contracts Manager, I told him about my return trip.

"Are you off your head?" he exclaimed, "You've just had a holiday romance that's all, pull yourself together, Sean. You've got a business to run."

I knew that what he was saying was true, and I knew that if I'd told anyone else they would have greeted me with the same response. But I didn't want to keep going back to my empty flat; working all hours, for … I couldn't even comprehend what I was working for. All I knew was that Thailand made me feel different, inspired me, made me feel enthused by life; and I wanted to feel that again.

A week later I was walking through those big glass doors at Bangkok airport once again, and Kim was waiting for me with that beautiful smile that I'd missed so inconceivably much. She ran into my arms and we started to kiss. She tasted even sweeter than I remembered.

"I've missed you, doctor Seany."

"I've missed you too, why do you think I'm here?" I laughed.

"I know a hotel in Bangkok, not too far from here," she said, typically already searching for a taxi.

We spent an amazing night together in Bangkok; my memories had deceived me, her skin was even softer to the touch, her hair even glossier than I'd recalled. Everything about her was perfection personified.

The next day we found ourselves back at Bangkok airport; we'd concocted a plan to fly out to Sámui Island. We'd negotiated some cheap flights and soon we were jetting off on the forty five minute journey to another breathtakingly stunning location. As we approached our accommodation I found myself wide mouthed in awe. A bungalow positioned right on the beach, looking out onto our own piece of beach heaven. My Bond girl had her movie star setting; we were both experiencing a millionaire's lifestyle all for the ridiculous price of £20 a night.

We spent the evening entwined on our bed, inspired by the sound of the calm sea caressing the sand outside. We'd watched the sun set and we woke early to watch it rise. It was a world away from the view from my flat window back in Cannock, and as I breathed in the fresh air, laden with golden rays, I felt at peace. We walked further down the beach to a small ramshackle hut where we paid a few baht to hire a boat for the day; out at sea I donned my snorkel and dived in. Flashes of colour darted around me as I splashed around to find my equilibrium and then, as I settled into my breathing pattern my eyes opened wide to take in the beauty of the carefree fish, vivid in colour; striking. I followed their swirling patterns, diving deeper into the ocean. They swam in front of my mask, in an almost showbiz fashion, welcoming me into their world just as Kim had done. And as I rose to the surface to be greeted by Kim's face, alive with happiness, peering over the edge of the boat; I realised then that the feelings I felt for her were deeper than anything I'd ever known. Without question I was in love.

With one day left before we were due to fly back to Bangkok, Kim and I sat down together on some rocks that we'd made our own over the last two weeks. Hand in hand we sat in silence for some time, both clearly contemplating the end of yet another all too brief holiday spent together. Then spontaneously the silence was broken by song; it was Kim, her Thai words filled the air like a sweet birdsong.

"That's beautiful," I said, enchanted, "What's it about?"

Her eyes fell to the ground, "It's about a young girl, so in love with her boyfriend but her family won't let them be together."

I could see the sentiment of the song had touched her.

"So sad," I agreed.

I reached down for my video camera and switched it on to record the beautiful girl on the beautiful beach, singing the heartfelt song. A moment that captivated the feelings we were sharing and a moment I wanted to cherish forever.

That evening we took our dinner on the beach front; the charcoal grey night sky was dotted with the light of the stars and the delicate multi-coloured lights scattered across the length of the beach. The first few metres of the sea were visible but beyond that was an almost eerie blackness, only recognisable as sea from the sound of the rush of waves emanating from the darkness. The tranquil evening was only interrupted by the clicks and ticks of insects in the tall trees and the serene Thai music playing gently in the background. I looked across the candlelit table and my heart pounded; I felt like it was burst through my chest if I didn't say what was surging through my vocal cords rushing to get out.

44

"Kim, I know now that I love you." I swallowed hard. "Would you like to spend your life with me?" I took a deep breath, "Would you like to marry me?" I didn't wait for a reply, "Kim, you could come and live in England; we can still come back to Thailand so you can see your family, and you can speak to them on the phone every day." I was working it all out in my head as I spoke. Then I realised she hadn't given me an answer. I paused.

"Yes Sean, I would like that a lot," she grinned.

"So, is that a yes?"

"Yes, doctor Seany," Kim said smiling, "I want to spend my life with you."

Her words surged through my body, and filled me with an unprecedented joy.

The next day we were back in Bangkok, saying our goodbyes, but this time was different. This time I was flying home the luckiest bloke alive. Kim's tears still ran like rivers down her cheeks, despite me repeatedly sweeping my thumb under her streaming eyes.

It was devastating to walk away from her, my fiancée, but I knew that as soon as was feasibly possible we would be together, as man and wife. Walking towards the security desk at Bangkok airport I turned to see her still standing, isolated from the crowd, looking lost without me. It broke my heart. I lifted my hand to my face and pushed the corners of my mouth up in a forced smile.

"Keep smiling," I shouted back, before walking away from my soul mate.

Back in the UK I knew I had to make my first port of call my parents' house. I wasn't sure how I would break the news to them, or what their reaction would be; I hoped they would be able to see just by looking at me, how happy Kim made me, and how hollow my life was without her.

When I arrived, my son Robbie was there having dinner; I wasn't expecting to have to break it to him as well but I willed them all to understand. The conversation was one-sided to say the least. My news wasn't greeted with squeals of excitement or hardy handshakes. Mum and Dad were silent, they listened and nodded. I didn't think it was wise to try and push it with them so I chose to let it sink in. Robbie couldn't help but speak up though;

"Are you mad, dad?" I expected that. "What are you doing? Did you fall and hit your head while you were out there?"

I put my arm round his shoulder, "Don't worry, I know what I'm doing."

He ribbed me for a while and then his mind wandered away and the awkward questioning stopped.

I knew mum and dad had more to say but they clearly weren't prepared to voice it there and then, so I made my way back home. I'd been in less than twenty minutes when the phone rang.

"Sean; it's mum."

"Hello, mum," I said, sensing an awkwardness in her tone.

"Sean, are you doing the right thing?" she questioned, in the sensitive way that only a mother could without sounding too judgemental.

"Yes, I know I am. You will love, Kim, she is the nicest person you will ever meet," I reassured.

Mum sighed, "Well it's your life; you're old enough to look after yourself," she hesitated, "It's just a shame I won't be there to see you get married."

I knew mum would never fly all that way. I'd already thought about that one, but deep down my wedding was about spending the rest of my life with Kim, I wasn't worried about lots of guests or a big party, I just wanted to stand arm in arm with my bride.

And so the arrangements began for January 1st 2006; our wedding day. The first day of the rest of our lives.

Chapter 6 – A Monk's Blessing

I couldn't get back to Bangkok quick enough, and once again through those big glass doors, the gateway between happiness and loneliness, I was reunited with my soul mate. I pulled her into my chest, almost crushing her in the process, but it was the only way to convey my feelings. The relief, the love, the joy. As I released her from my embrace I noticed a man standing sheepishly beside her.

"This is my cousin," Kim introduced him as soon as our eyes met. "He's a policeman in Bangkok, he wanted to meet you," she continued.

I put my hand out to meet his and he shook it with vigour.

"Hello, nice to meet you," I said.

He looked straight into my eyes, "Yes, hello," he replied still gripping my hand.

Bloody hell, he's a friendly chap, I thought to myself.

"He's booked us a nice hotel, so we can stay for a night before we go to my village in Udon," Kim grinned.

Kim's village was in Thani, north of Bangkok, I didn't fancy doing anymore travelling so a night in a hotel sounded perfect to me.

"Well what are we waiting for, let's go!" I said urging Kim to lead the way.

The hotel was only a short taxi ride away, we went straight up to our room; I took a shower and then settled down for the night. It had been a long journey and I was more than happy to simply lay down with my fiancée. I don't know what time I dozed off but when I peeled open my bleary eyes the next morning, Kim was already up and dressed and had arranged a car to take us to her village. I knew Kim lived quite a distance from Bangkok but I wasn't prepared for the 9 hour journey that ensued that day. As we travelled I watched the sun rise to its peak, shocking my system yet again into an overdose of sweat and discomfort. And then I watched it fall, to be replaced by a brilliant white moon, its power emanating in the sky above. We stopped for a brief moment to pick up Kim's friend, Nee, then continued on our way for another hour or so. Entering Kim's village I wasn't sure what to expect, the road tapered off into more of a dirt track, there were no street lights, the surroundings only faintly illuminated by flickers of light coming from the huts either side of the track. I could just about make out silhouettes of people, dozens of faceless bodies busying themselves both inside and outside of the huts. The car came to an abrupt halt outside of a small hut on the right of the track. I opened the door nervously.

Nee sensed my uncertainty, "Don't worry Sean, you'll be ok," she said comfortingly.

I'd barely got both feet out of the car when people came flooding out of the hut to meet me. I was overwhelmed, not least because I couldn't work out how so many people could fit inside a, I thought about it, a shed! My eyes began to adjust to the dim light and I could make out features, smiles, bright eyes, excitedly touching my skin, stroking my hair. It was a surreal moment, an almost out of body experience. I'd seen outsiders greeted like this on television documentaries, but I didn't think that little old Sean would be afforded the same welcome. The excitement bubbled into loud laughter and joking, I looked to Kim for reassurance. I didn't really have a clue what was happening, but Kim's kind nod told me I was doing the right thing.

She let the excitement die down and then took my hand to lead me into her home. We walked through the opening, a far cry from a secure front door, and I was blown away by the vision I met. In the main room, more bodies sat gathered on the floor in a circle, in the middle of them were dishes and dishes of traditional foods, I could almost see the flavours rising up from the small bowls and sweeping around the circle of Kim's family.

Two of the younger women made a space for Kim and I to join the ring and we sat down to eat. I'd silently hoped that Kim's family would be welcoming and that they'd be happy with Kim's choice of husband, but this celebration was beyond all expectations. Generations upon generations of Kim's family had come out to meet me and all seemed happy that I was there. And I was more than happy to be there. The girl to my left offered me a dish of noodles; I looked on, spying something that looked suspiciously fiery flickering between the snake-like twists. I hesitated, not wanting to be rude, "Errm, I don't like spicy food," I said as politely as possible.

Kim laughed out loud, "Don't worry, my family know you have a baby mouth."

"Thank you," I said, slightly embarrassed but glad I wouldn't be caught out.

One of the men passed me a beer, while the women proceeded to pass round and serve up the magnificent spread of food. Throughout the evening I had every need attended to, the women all jumping over one another to make sure I was comfortable, with my cushions seemingly being plumped and adjusted every five minutes. Music blasted out and the volume of the bouncing chatter gradually increased to compensate. People came from across the village to meet me, I felt like royalty. And once the hut was full guests were happy to stand outside and join in the party. I couldn't understand much of what was being said but I could tell from their actions and from the warm buzz in the room that they were talking about our wedding and the future that lay in store for Kim back in England.

The celebrations and planning went on late into the night and eventually Kim and I found an opportunity to sneak off into a side room to bed down for the night. I felt as if I'd only been sleeping a matter of minutes when the unmistakable sound of chickens shrieked through the hut and woke me up. My eyes opened instantly, and I lay for a moment taking in everything that was going on around me. All the people that had welcomed me the night before were seemingly still there, and they were still moving frantically in and out of the hut and in and out of the room where I'd been sleeping. Kim too was up and working, she saw the shell shocked look on my face and came to my side, stroking my head tenderly she said, "Everyone is getting ready for the wedding, you have to get ready Sean, everyone is coming."

"Ok, ok," I said, enchanted by her excitement. "Where do I shower?"

Kim held my hand and walked me out of the hut into another smaller hut a few metres from the main house; this one really was the size of a small shed, and inside a bucket of water sat poised to wake me up with a shock.

I think the whole village heard my screams as I 'showered', and I clearly amused them all as each scream was greeted with raucous laughter.

I returned to the main hut to find Kim had laid out my clothes for our big day. She'd organised it all and she'd made an excellent choice; a smart white suit with a red Thai band that hung over my shoulder, across my body and down to my waist. Putting it on I felt very emotional, I knew that I was just hours away from marrying the woman of my dreams, but I was doing it without any of my friends and family around me. As I looked in the mirror at my reflection I spotted the swarms of Kim's family still rushing past with flowers and platters of food; I smiled to myself, realising that Kim's family more than made up for my absentees.

While I waited for Kim to get ready I played outside with Kim's nephews. They were only little but they were fascinated by the colour of my skin; Doctor Seany, as everyone had taken to calling me, was a real novelty.

After a while the hubbub that had been the norm for the morning almost instantly died down, I looked round to see that the monk had arrived and was being welcomed into the hut. I quickly dropped the football we'd been kicking around and followed behind him.

I walked in and caught sight of the future Mrs Felton, dressed in an elegant cream dress, her long black locks scooped neatly up off her shoulders, she looked like a porcelain doll. My eyes fixed on her, unable, unwilling to notice anyone else. She smiled in reply to my appreciative look and signalled for me to sit next to her. The main room was full once again, but I made my way through the well wishers and sat down as she'd directed. In front of us was a small bush positioned ceremoniously in place, it was adorned with white bands, which the wedding guests took turns to remove from the bush and tie around each of our wrists. All the while the monk, who was yet to acknowledge me, stood chanting and singing. After each band was tied, the giver would kneel down in front of us and pray, I assumed they were praying for our future happiness, but as I looked across at Kim I was convinced that we didn't need prayers, we were made for each other.

People came and came, familiar faces, new faces, all of them smiling, all of them sharing in our love. The monk turned his attention to me and proceeded to throw water over me as part of a blessing; once again I became the centre of amusement as our guests laughed at my shock. I was glad that although heaped in ceremony, prayer and tradition, our wedding day was still full of fun and laughter, something that symbolised our relationship from the start.

"What's happening now," I whispered to Kim as people started to come forward again.

"They're putting money in that bowl; it's for us, Sean, so we keep money in our lives," she whispered back.

I laughed, "I like this bit; can we get married every day?" I joked.

With the ceremony complete we went on to enjoy a jovial reception; halfway through I took a moment to catch my breath, and to appreciate my wife. I looked over to her, so clearly loved by all of her friends and family, and so dearly loved by me. Every cliché in the book rushed through my head; luckiest man alive, dream come true; all of them were applicable and all of them smeared a gleaming smile on my face and filled my heart with hope.

That night Kim's cousin drove us to a hotel so that we could spend our first night as man and wife in comfort.

"Good morning, Mrs Felton," I said as Kim slowly roused the next day.

"Good morning, Doctor Seany," she said coyly.

Our honeymoon continued with a trip back to Sámui Island, the place where I'd proposed just a few months earlier. Kim and I didn't leave each other's sides, we were typical honeymooners, but with the added intensity brought by the knowledge that I would be going back to the UK without her.

After two glorious weeks we travelled back to Bangkok airport where I was to catch my connecting flight back home. Kim had travelled in silence almost all the way back there; I could tell she was as distraught as I was about our imminent separation.

"It's ok, we'll be together again soon; if the embassy needs anything else from me I can email it to them," I said pressing enough money into her hand to allow her to arrange her visa. "Please Kim, don't worry, it will all be ok."

The tears fell for both of us as we turned and went our separate ways. I couldn't believe I was walking away from my beautiful bride.

Chapter 7 – Secrets of the past

I flew back to the UK filled with an all consuming happiness, wretched with a painful feeling of emptiness. Our wedding day had been more than I'd ever dreamed it could be and the time we'd spent together on our honeymoon was simply magical. But now I ached to be with Kim, to have my wife by my side.

It was a typical April day when Kim arrived at Birmingham airport. The morning had started bright and crisp but by the afternoon, just as her plane was about to land, the April showers fell relentlessly. But nothing could dampen the happiness and joy that I felt as she walked through the arrivals gate. I swept her up in my arms and proudly walked through the airport hand in hand with my wife. In the car on the way back to Heath Hayes, Kim seemed anxious, her silence betraying her inner thoughts, I reached across and tenderly held her hand, squeezing it gently as I drove, my way of reassuring her that all would be ok.

"It's a long journey back to my apartment, Kim," I said, not sure exactly what was bothering her.

"I'll run you a nice hot bath when we get home, darling. Then you can really relax and unwind."

I was excited to show Kim my home, it was a two bedroom ground floor flat, I'd lived there for four years and I loved it. The garden had been recently seen to, and was looking immaculate. I hoped Kim would find it homely, the perfect haven for our marriage to start.

We pulled up outside and Kim peered out of the steamy car window. Her face a blank canvas of reaction. She said nothing. I grabbed her bags from the boot and showed her indoors.

"Welcome to your new home," I announced eagerly.

Kim still remained silent. Her eyes explored the room, her head remaining stationary for the whole exploration.

The motionless, silent, solemn Kim stood in my front room, was far from the smiling Kim that I knew and loved.

"Are you ok?" I asked anxiously.

"Yes Sean, I'm just very tired," she replied, still devoid of emotion.

"I'll run you that bath I promised," I said cheerily, ushering her over to the sofa, "You sit yourself down and relax."

Kim sat down, but looked far from relaxed as I left the room to run her bath.

She stayed in the bathroom for hours; I assumed she was just unwinding after the long journey and emotional upheaval. Looking out of the flat window I could appreciate how she might have been feeling a little bit homesick, the grey skyline doing nothing to inspire or warm the cockles. Eventually she stepped out of the bathroom; I looked on anticipating her beaming smile but it didn't come.

"It's ok, love, I've been out and got you a rice cooker and some rice, and chicken, well there's all sorts for you to eat here."

"Thank you, Sean," she simply replied.

I tried not to read too much into it, tiredness can affect people in different ways, I thought as we started to prepare our first meal together. Stir fried chicken and rice; our first meal as man and wife in our Cannock home. The conversation was stilted but the food was perfect, and the vision sat across the table was as beautiful as the day we'd met. The travel had taken its toll on us both and an early night was calling both of us. Snuggled together in our marital bed was all I'd dreamt about for months, but I only managed to cherish the moment for a few minutes before falling fast asleep. But something stirred me in the middle of the night; I reached over to cuddle up to my wife, only for my hand to meet a lifeless cold sheet. I opened my eyes and sat up simultaneously, double checking with my mind that the whole evening hadn't been a stunningly vivid dream. And then I heard her, faint sobs coming from the other room. I jumped out of bed and ran to the doorway of the front room. My poor Kim looked up from the sofa her face desperately sad and streaked with the contours of the tears that must have been flowing for hours.

"What's up, Kim? What happened? Are you alright?" I sat down beside her as I spoke and she flung her arms around me before I could finish.

Her sobbing was no longer muffled; it burnt through my ears and scorched my heart.

"What has happened?" I pleaded again, "Please tell me; it'll be ok, don't worry." Still Kim just cried. I cradled her back to the bedroom and we got back into bed. As I lay back down Kim started rubbing her finger slowly up and down my back. Her delicate touch seemed to be soothing both of us and eventually her sobbing ceased.

"I've got something to tell you, Sean," she said in a tone that made me roll over instantly, not sure what to expect. Then she raised her hand up in front of her face.

"Look," was all she said.

I strained my eyes to try and focus on whatever it was I was supposed to be looking at but the lack of light made it impossible to see anything. I reached to my bedside table and switched on the small lamp, and as I turned back to Kim I saw what she was showing me. Her hand shook as she held it up to reveal only four digits and a barren gap above the knuckle where the fifth should have been. I gasped in response. In the confusion I assumed she'd somehow done in there and then,

"How have you done that?" I blurted, not registering that there wasn't any blood and therefore wasn't a fresh wound.

"I did it on the farm putting rice in the machine," she wept.

"How didn't I know about this?" I said, horrified. "I rang you every day and you didn't tell me, Kim."

"I can't remember much about it, I fell asleep when it happened," she cried.

My heart strained for her, "Kim, don't worry about anything, I love you and having your finger missing is not going to change that, I promise," I said kissing both her hands.

The next morning I noticed Kim still looked uneasy about her revelation.

"Don't be scared, Kim, you're safe now, don't worry about your finger; I'm a doctor remember?" I joked. At last she broke a faint smile.

I'd made plans for the day, and after breakfast I took Kim to visit some of my family, she went down a treat. I knew they would all love her as much as I did. She was the courteous sweet girl that I'd fallen in love with and they were compelled to love her. After doing the rounds with the family I took her on a shopping spree; Kim wasn't quite prepared for the cold, wet April we were in the midst of and didn't hold back when it came to snapping up some warmer layers in the high street stores. Then for the next few days we hauled ourselves up in our flat and enjoyed the start of our married life together.

The weekend came and went in a blur of laughter, eating and romance, and as Monday morning came around I prepared to get back to work.

"You'll be ok, Kim," I said as my nervous bride stood swamped by the door frame. "You have my number, if you need anything just call me; I'm not far."

And to start with she did call me, a lot! But as her confidence grew and her knowledge of her new hometown blossomed, Kim began to make friends and found she settled easily into the unexpectedly close community of Thai women that were living in the area. The women would all meet up and chat on a regular basis; it made me so happy to see that Kim was settling in and building a life for herself.

"Kim, what do you think about getting a little job?" I asked her one day over dinner. It had occurred to me that although she was settling in well with the Thai community, the English community was still relatively alien to her. "Perhaps you could help out at a charity or something? You'd make lots of new friends."

"Yes I'd like that Sean," she replied, seemingly grateful that I'd made the suggestion. And with that I went about arranging for someone from the local college to come and visit her; they discussed the options open to her and agreed that she could get a job at the local charity shop.

Kim was excited about her first day of work, babbling at a rate of knots as we walked to the shop together for her first shift. We were greeted by a kind elderly lady, with ashen grey hair that framed her face in a soft bob; she welcomed Kim in enthusiastically, clearly fascinated by the exotic woman that stood before her.

"Come in dear, please," she said, grinning almost unnaturally at Kim, who beamed back.

"Let me show you where to put your things and then I'll get you a nice cup of tea; you do drink tea I take it?" she asked awkwardly.

"Yes, I do, thank you very much," Kim said with her usual politeness. I felt very proud and left the shop confident that she was in good hands.

Kim loved her first day and came home full of stories about the customers in the shop and their strange mannerisms. She was really making a go of her new role, she'd found her niche. But a few weeks later it all came crashing to an end. I arrived home to find Kim sat on the edge of our bed crying wearily.

"What on earth's happened?" I said rushing to be by her side.

"The man in the shop," she wept, "He has been touching me."

I froze, paralysed by anger and a need to protect her. "What do you mean?" I eventually managed to utter.

Kim told me exactly what had happened and my blood coursed through my veins like mercury. "Leave it with me," I managed calmly. And with that I got up and rang the college and told our contact exactly what happened to Kim. She was as horrified as I was and she assured me it would be dealt with.

"I don't want to go back there Sean," Kim said timidly; I laughed at her suggestion.

"Of course you don't, and there's no way you ever are," I reassured her.

Kim soon picked herself up after her rocky initiation into employment. She found another job with a local packing company once I'd managed to sort out all of her papers, and she really began to enjoy her English life, slotting into the nine to five with relative ease.

After a few weeks I surprised Kim with the news that we were taking a holiday back to Thailand; her face positively glowed with excitement. As the plane neared Thailand I could almost feel the spark firing back up inside her soul; she loved her family dearly and I was pleased that she still had the opportunity to see them, even if it was only for a holiday.

It was a blissful time; her family all fussed around me, treating me like royalty yet again; I was humbled by their acceptance and kindness. But the trip was marred slightly by Kim being unwell; I worried that it was the switch back to the rich Thai food, that perhaps the blandness of her English diet had somehow weakened her stomach, she looked pale and tired, and by the end of the holiday I could see she wasn't capable of many more tourist trips or visits to her extended family members.

"You need to see a doctor when we get back, Kim," I said as she returned from her third trip to the aeroplane toilet.

Kim couldn't even reply, she just nodded, putting a tissue to her mouth to try and hold back anymore sickness. I watched over her all the way home as she sipped water, slept and then rushed down the aisle to be sick once more.

The day after we landed in England Kim made an appointment with the GP.

"I'm coming with you my love, there's something really wrong here."

"I'll be fine Sean," she protested.

"I just want to come anyway; just to make sure you understand everything the doctor says." Kim's English was actually pretty good by now, but I couldn't help but worry about her. We sat anxiously in the doctor's waiting room; neither of us able to deflect the worry by flicking through the stack of antique women's magazines.

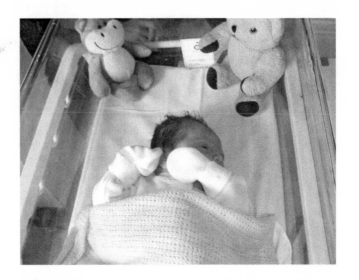

"Mrs Felton?" The doctor's voice called out from the corridor behind us.

We stood up and walked hand in hand in the direction of the voice.

In his consulting room Kim methodically explained her symptoms; the doctor duly listened and scribbled notes on a scrap of paper in front of him. Neither of us had expected the diagnosis we left the doctor's with that afternoon.

Kim was pregnant.

I'd never even considered having anymore children; I'd always envisaged Robbie as my only child. Kim and I had never discussed it, and yet it was clear that we were both elated by the thought. Our own little baby.

We both thrived during the pregnancy, the anticipation of the birth consumed our every waking moment. Well that and trying to renovate a house that I'd bought. While the renovations were underway we rented a small bungalow in Penkridge, not far from

Cannock, and I worked around the clock to try and get it ready in time for us to move in as a family of three. But the baby just beat me to it; on July 26th 2007 Jobe Matthew Reginald Felton was born weighing 7 pound 10 oz. He was a healthy bundle of jet black hair and edible smiles. And one month later we moved into our plush new family home; the three of us; the Felton family. And as I looked on at Jobe lying peacefully in his crib and Kim resting contentedly on the sofa, I felt undefeatable; I had a real family and at that moment nothing else in the world mattered.

Chapter 8 – Memories in the mist

Christmas of 2007 felt magical; as I sat surrounded by my family, Kim working merrily in the kitchen to prepare the Christmas dinner, and Robbie making his little brother giggle in front of the dressed tree, I felt a very proud man. But despite the blissful Christmas, as the New Year set in things took a turn for the worst. Work began to slow up and I had to battle to get the money that was owed to me from the little work I had been lucky enough to get. The stress piled on and the bills piled up and within a few months I was forced to look at closing down the company. I moved the office back to our home, hoping I could save a bit of money there; I even went out on the tools myself to try and bring in some extra cash.

"It'll be ok Sean," Kim said one evening, noticing the tension compounding in my worried brow.

"I know love; we just need to be careful with our spending at the moment. It'll pick up soon," I said fixing my most optimistic face in her direction.

Kim was happy with that, I felt reassured that she was so understanding about the downturn. And despite our money worries Kim remained the bubbly and vivacious woman who made me thankful every time I looked at her. She'd made lots of friends, mostly Thai people; as new people came into the area the Thai community always rallied together to make them feel welcome, Kim included. I would come home on many occasions to find Kim had invited some fellow Thais round for an evening meal. I could tell that being around Thai people was good for her, and I made a conscious effort to go to the local Thai temple in Lichfield, she always seemed to have a new found passion for life when she'd been.

"Sean, you'll never guess who's coming?" she said one evening, jumping up and down in front of me like an excited child.

"Erm, no I won't, but I suggest you tell me before you burst," I laughed.

"Nee! Nee is coming!" she squealed. "She's bringing her boyfriend, and they're coming to England and they're coming here, Seany."

Kim hugged me, the thought of seeing her dearest friend was clearly overwhelming for her.

And when we collected her from the airport the reunion of the two women was beautiful. We spent a magnificent week together; we forgot the troubles with money and the business and we just enjoyed the time we had with them. It felt good to be carefree and Kim was permanently elated, giggling and chatting with Nee, long into the night, every night.

But as the age old cruel twist of life dictated, the good times came to an end upon Nee's return home. Kim was sullen, withdrawn, as if she was in mourning.

"Are you ok Kim?" I asked after another evening of relative silence.

"Yes," she huffed, "Just a bit home sick. I miss Thailand," she said thoughtfully.

"Well we might be able to go back there towards the end of the year," I suggested rather spontaneously. I hated seeing Kim upset; I would do anything to make her happy and I knew that going back to Thailand would be the only way to put her smile back on her face.

By July, Kim, Joe and I were boarding the plane for Joe's first long haul flight to Thailand. From the moment we landed I could see the relief in Kim's face, but it was short lived. Joe was unwell, we knew the flight would be difficult for him but there was something else not quite right, and our holiday was put on hold as we rushed him to the nearest hospital. The doctors there were very helpful and confirmed that he was suffering quite badly with tonsillitis; they gave him an injection to jumpstart the healing process and after a few days he was back to his old self, making the most of the hotel pool. As I splashed around with him and pulled him around on his inflatable I looked across at a distant Kim lying on the poolside. She looked positively disinterested; in the pool, in Joe, in me. I tried to ignore it, perhaps I'm just being paranoid, I thought to myself, perhaps she's just savouring being back home? I wasn't sure what it was but by the time we were getting ready for dinner the distance felt cavernous.

"Kim, have I upset you?" the words came out despite being convinced I'd done nothing wrong.

"No," came the succinct reply.

"Why are you not yourself, Kim? What's up?"

"Nothing," she replied not offering anything more in her defence.

I chose not to push it and that night as I lay silently next to my wife I felt as if I was lying next to a total stranger.

As the holiday went on she spent more and more time conversing in Thai, accentuating the isolation that was already suffocating me. I decided not to let it get to me, I wanted to give Joe a magnificent holiday, I was adamant we were going to enjoy ourselves even if Kim wasn't interested, and I ploughed through the next couple of weeks drawing on every ounce of my English determination.

Back in the UK, the silent treatment persisted, our relationship was breaking down before my eyes and I couldn't work out why.

"Please Kim, just tell me what's wrong and I can fix it; I'm a doctor remember."

"It's nothing, I'm just cold."

"But you were like this in Thailand and you weren't cold then?"

"And nobody will speak to me over here," she continued.

"But everyone talks to you; you've got lots of friends."

"No Sean, I haven't, and we don't ever go anywhere," she continued sulkily.

"But Kim, I try my best, I've just taken you to Thailand! I didn't want to argue with her, but I couldn't believe what she was saying; it just wasn't true.

"I don't have the money like I used to Kim, please understand," I urged before looking across at Joe playing happily on the floor, "We do have Joe to look after as well," I said trying to diffuse the situation.

Kim just rolled her eyes and breathed a heavy breath that said it all.

Days went by and Kim and I barely spoke, I enjoyed going out to work as it gave me the opportunity to get away from her disapproving, disappointed eyes.

It was a Thursday afternoon, 2 o'clock, and I'd forgotten my phone. I'd managed all morning without it but I took advantage of a moment of down time to pop home and pick it up. I walked through the front door.

"I'm home!" I yelled.

Nothing.

"Kim, are you there?"

Nothing. She must have popped out I thought to myself, then I heard something that sent a surge of panic through my veins. Joe was crying upstairs. I took the stairs two at a time, belting up them in horror. I burst into his room to meet a vision I never thought possible. Joe was alone in the cot. Joe had been left alone in the house. I swept him up in my arms, the palm of my hand cradling his precious head as I cuddled him into my chest.

"Oh Joe, my poor baby."

As the realisation of the moment swept over me I leant against the bedroom wall to steady myself. How could she just leave him?

His crying soon settled but I couldn't help but wonder how long he'd been wailing and there'd been no-one there to soothe him. Ten minutes later the front door opened. I instantly felt rage.

"Where have you been! What are you doing?" I'd never felt an anger like it.

Kim looked blankly back at me, "What?"

I coughed in disgust, "Kim, you can't leave Joe on his own, we don't do that in the UK, we'll get into trouble," I paused to consider the consequences, "They'll take him off us!"

Kim's face was a picture of nonchalance.

"Please don't do that again Kim, anything could have happened, he needs you to be there for him." I couldn't believe I had to state the obvious to his own mother.

Kim just looked at me, like a petulant teenager, almost disbelieving. I half expected her to say, "whatever".

I went back to work hoping that the seriousness of the situation had sunk in, despite her obvious disdain at being told the error of her ways. I rushed home early that evening just to be sure, and when I did I was greeted by a very welcome sight of Kim and Joe singing songs together on the lounge rug. I bent down and kissed them both on the forehead; I wasn't one to hold a grudge, and I'd managed to calm myself down over the course of the afternoon; I'd even convinced myself that the whole incident was just a massive cultural difference and, well no harm had been done.

I didn't mention the incident again but still something grated on her; my wife became an acquaintance and our family home felt like lodgings for both of us. The tangible distance got greater with each day.

I hadn't given up on our marriage though and I was determined to make Kim smile again, one evening she came down from putting Joe to bed and sat down next to me on the sofa.

"Sean," she mewed, "My sister's friend has some land for sale near our village in Thailand."

"Oh right," I said with interest.

"It's very cheap Sean, we could buy it, it's good land."

For the first time in months I could see a spark of excitement in Kim's eyes, I wanted it to stay and as we spoke more the plot of land sounded like a perfect investment opportunity. Business had picked up a bit and there was some money in the house and so over the next few days I arranged for a loan against the house.

"But Kim, this does mean we won't actually be able to go to Thailand for a few years as I'll need all our money to pay the loan back," I said as I signed the final paper.

"It's ok, no problem," she said, "My sister will arrange everything."

And with that the wheels were set in motion for us to buy the land, build a house there and then retire to the land of smiles and sunshine. We'd both found that spark that we were lacking, we were both excited; I knew I'd have to work hard but I'd never been afraid of hard work and I'd always been determined to achieve my goals. And what better goal than a life in paradise with my family and a homestead back in England for the times when I missed the grey skies and crisp autumn mornings. Kim told her friends about our great plans but none of them seemed to share our positivity, I wasn't quite sure why they weren't as supportive as we'd hoped but despite their sneering Kim spent more and more time with them. Abandoning her home life to live the life of a carefree young woman didn't sit well with me. Of course I wanted her to be happy, more than anything in the world, and I wanted her to have friends but I never imagined that my wife would be out at night till the early hours of the morning, partying with people I didn't really know, while I stayed at home tending to Joe. I sometimes questioned whether I resented her antics through jealousy of her free spirit, but the answer to that question was always no, I knew that I didn't want to go out, all I wanted was a happy family life, content with the simple things.

Our differences of opinion inevitably led to arguments. I couldn't see the draw, what could possibly be so great out there that would mean you could leave your son and husband for hours at a time, without even a heartbeat of uncertainty. Our rows never achieved an outcome other than days of Kim holding on tight to those grudges that she harboured. The way she glared at me, almost in repulsion I felt as if I'd committed murder not asked her to stay home to put her son to bed. And with me playing mum, dad, businessman and housekeeper, life was getting tough, and Kim seemed to be making it tougher.

"I want to go back to Thailand to see my family," she announced as I set foot through the front door after another gruelling day.

I dropped my bag to the hallway floor and breathed a tired sigh, "We can't afford it, Kim. We have to pay for the land now, remember, I haven't got a money tree."

She scowled at me then muttered something in Thai under her breath as she walked away. As I stood bemused I wondered how such a beautiful poetic language could sound so contorted with anger.

The evening was spent as most evenings were, in silence. How had our relationship come to this, I thought, pouring myself a much needed short once I'd put Joe to bed. I flopped down into the armchair and slowly massaged my temples to try to ease some of the strain. I closed my eyes and as I did the living room door burst open to allow a group of Kim's friends to come spilling in, noisily jabbering away in Thai.

"Oh hi," I said politely, "I didn't know you were coming round."

A mumbled hello came from a couple of the guys but the women in the group said nothing, they could barely even hold my gaze. They seemed nervous, and that made me nervous. Kim stepped forward, shooing me away and pulling them further into my house. And so I left her to it, retreating to the kitchen whilst strangers commandeered my front room. I managed to pick up my drink before the door was slammed in my face.

I felt uncomfortable.   I could sense something wasn't quite right. Those that could look at me had a suggestion of something hidden behind their eyes, and those that couldn't obviously had a more powerful conscience. Sat at the kitchen table I looked towards the lounge, where, from behind the shut door, I could hear the crescendo and diminuendo of voices, they sounded conspiratorial. I thought back to the warnings

71

that people had given me about Thai women, I shook it off, Kim was different; I wouldn't have fallen for her if she wasn't. I threw my drink back down my throat, the slight burn as it went down soothed my mind and I decided to get an early night. I walked towards the lounge door to say goodnight to our guests, but placing my hand on the handle I reconsidered. Somehow I felt my courtesy wouldn't be welcomed, so I turned away and trudged upstairs to drift off to sleep alone.

Chapter 9 – Secrets and Strangers

Most of Kim's friends had become British citizens over recent months but Kim's application was repeatedly refused. She was going to college, sitting English exams doing everything she could to try and prove her commitment to the country. I knew she felt persecuted and I felt it for her; we just wanted to be a British family, I secretly hoped that citizenship would make her feel more at peace, and help her to enjoy her family life again. But it didn't come, and Kim started directing her anger about the situation towards me. More and more arguments ensued and more and more covert discussions with her friends occurred. Covert in the sense that they were carried out in Thai and delivered with stealth like mannerisms but entirely conspicuous in the fact that they were carried out in my presence, with eyes slyly moving in my direction and heads drawing closer together as they discussed whatever it was they were discussing.

My head spun with ideas about what they could possibly be talking about. All I wanted was a normal family life;

"It's not much to ask," I said out loud one morning as my voice spilled outside of my mind.

"What isn't?" Kim asked; she was cheerier than normal.

"Oh nothing," I replied, shocked by her light hearted tone.

"Oh right, well never mind that, my friend has invited us to the circus, Sean," Kim chirped.

"Really?"

"Yes, she's got free tickets, shall we go?"

"Yes that sounds great, Joe will love it," I grinned. Finally we would be going out as a proper family.

That evening we arrived at the circus tent early; I didn't want Joe to miss a second of it, and I wanted to make the most of being out with my wife. We loitered by the popcorn stand waiting for the main doors to open.

"There she is," Kim said, pointing towards her friend who was walking towards us.

I squinted my eyes, I didn't recognise the man she was with but I knew it wasn't her husband. Before I had a chance to question it the couple were with us and exchanging greetings. I didn't catch his name but the conversation moved on quickly and I missed my opportunity to ask again.

The couple conversed mostly in Thai, leaving me, as usual, to try and hone it on the few words I'd picked up over the years, although my novice vocabulary never seemed to stretch to a full sentence; and whilst I tried to fill in the blanks in my half translated phrases, my mind began to wander. Who was he? Why hadn't Kim mentioned that she wasn't coming with her husband? And as the questions kept rolling something strange happened; the man reached his hand behind him and pulled his brown leather wallet from his back pocket; I could tell it was leather; soft and malleable as he thumbed open the clasp that held it together. And as the clasp popped he revealed a ream of notes that suggested he needed armed security walking behind him. I thought maybe he was just getting some money out to buy some popcorn but instead he just stood there, flashing the cash in front of Kim. What's he playing at, I thought to myself, surely he's not trying to impress her right under my nose. After an awkward exchange of glances he slowly closed the wallet, pressed it shut and returned it to his back pocket, emphasising the tight squeeze to try and fit it all in. I shrugged it off as I saw the doors were opening to allow us to take our seats for the show.

We walked in the big top and I headed straight for the front row.

"Joe is going to love this," I declared.

"Can't we sit back there?" Kim said pointing to seats three rows back, which just happened to house Mr Moneybags.

"No, we're right at the front here, Joe will be able to see everything; we're not moving," I said determined to put my foot down. My point was a valid one but not the most pertinent. I didn't trust the stranger whose eyes I could feel boring into the back of my head. Kim just looked at me, and untypically didn't argue the point.

"Good evening ladies and gentleman," the circus master roared.

Joe bounced on my lap in excitement. The music and lights danced energetically around us and Joe's eyes opened to take in the spectacle. He squeezed my hand tightly each time something more amazing and more invigorating happened. Alternating between giggles and squeals he was clearly in his element. And so was I. Nothing made me happier than seeing Joe happy, and this impromptu trip to the circus was doing just that; I turned to see if Kim's friend was enjoying herself but when I looked back I noticed that Mr Moneybags was sat on his own. I looked down the length of the row, stopping at each face to try and spot her. Curiosity got the better of me and I allowed my eyes to search each row until I found her. Eventually I did, on the other side of the circus tent; I watched her for a moment, seemingly not interested in the acrobats flipping and vaulting furiously in front of her. What on earth was going on?

Another squeal from Joe ended my analysis and I was back enjoying the magic that the show was creating. As we piled out of the tent Kim made her way towards her friend who was now reunited with the strange man. The three said a brief goodbye while I stopped to do up Joe's jacket. And then we made our way back home in silence.

In bed that night my suspicious mind just kept ticking over; what was with the man with the cash? Why weren't they sitting together? What has Kim been talking to her friends about in all her not so secret meetings? It was a Poirot mystery revealing itself in my own life and I couldn't for the life of me work out who did it, or even what it was they had or hadn't done.

I needed to ask the main character and so I rolled over and cautiously reached an arm around Kim, cuddling up behind her.

"Kim, can you tell me what's going on please?" I asked calmly. "Why didn't your friend come with her husband and why didn't they sit together, and why was he flashing his money at you?"

"What's wrong with you," Kim snapped, shrugging my arm away. "We've had a good night so why do you have to spoil it? There's nothing going on; you're thinking wrong, Sean," she finished crossly.

Hmm perhaps that was the wrong line of questioning I thought, I rolled back over, still thoughtful but willing to let it lie for now.

The next day I tried with attempt number two.

"Kim, there's something going on, I want to know what; it's not right, I'm your husband and we have Joe, there shouldn't be any secrets."

She looked at me thoughtfully. "Ok, I wasn't going to tell you but my friend is having an affair," she could tell I needed more, "With the man at the circus. Her husband does not treat her right. He has kicked her, Sean."

"But why did he flash his money at you?" I said not convinced that was the full story.

"He's just a show off; Sean, you don't have to worry, I am with you remember?" she said tenderly.

In that moment I felt like my old Kim was back. I wrapped my arms around her and kissed her passionately; thankful that it wasn't her that was straying.

"I don't want any trouble in this house though, Kim. I don't want her husband coming here and saying we've been hiding this from him," I looked into her eyes, "It's not right you know, Kim."

"Just forget about it Sean," she said, carefully avoiding my searching statement.

I tried to forget about it, but I wasn't comfortable with the knowing, especially when the philanderer came round to visit. I felt awkward being part of her secret, but thankfully within a few days it was all out in the open and she'd officially left her husband, who I felt nothing but pity for.

The following weekend I spotted her hand in hand with her new man, at least I thought it was him from a distance, but as we walked towards each other down the busy high street I realised that her new partner wasn't Mr Moneybags from the circus at all. Something didn't add up.

"So who is it then?" I asked Kim when I got home.

"The man from the circus; it's his cousin."

"What? So why didn't you tell me that from the start?" I asked, disgusted at all the lies that the affair of a relative stranger could evoke.

"I told you she was living with someone new," Kim replied sheepishly.

"This doesn't add up Kim, what the hell is going on?" I demanded.

"Why do you have to be so clever Sean; why do you ask so many questions?"

A blazing row ensued. I'd never felt so much rage; all I wanted was a simple honest life with my wife and son, and all I seemed to get was deceit and disrespect.

As round after round of fiery words were blasted in my direction I seethed in anger, and unable to take anymore I picked my dinner plate off the table and slammed it down on the floor. The shatter on the kitchen floor silenced us both. I'd reached my limit and stepping over the splintered pieces of porcelain I walked past Kim and out of the front door.

I wasn't sure where I was going but I needed that space to clear my head; I'd walked for about 5 minutes before I found myself in the corner shop asking the young girl behind the counter for some fags and a lighter. I hadn't smoked for two and a half years; my reason for stopping was Kim. She'd nagged and nagged about my smoking and eager to please I managed to curb my habit. But now, in a moment of defiance, I savoured that first lug of nicotine as it swept to the back of my throat and calmed my inner being. Blowing out the thick cloud of smoke that followed, I suddenly felt empowered to stand up for myself, to do what I wanted rather than trying to please the un-please-able.

I walked round the corner and perched myself on a small wooden bench, just outside the launderette. Drawing another hefty gasp on my cigarette the questions started flying around my head. Why does she keep lying to me? I've done everything I can for that girl, what's going on? And then came a thought I'd never wanted to consider; perhaps we should split up? But instantly a voice in my head replied; no, that would be terrible. I only saw Joe at weekends as it was, as I was working such long hours during the week, I couldn't bear the thought of seeing him even less. I'd missed out on so much with Robbie, I was determined history wouldn't repeat itself with Joe. I needed to make things work. I smoked the rest of the fag with a frightening intensity; soaking up its calming properties before I returned home.

And boy did I need them; back at the house Kim had initiated the silent treatment. And it lasted for days. Sunday came around and Robbie visited to join us for a Sunday lunch. But the silence across the dinner table was deafening. Kim didn't make any effort to call a truce for the sake of Robbie. After dinner Robbie and I went out into the garden where he asked the question he'd been dying to ask all day,

"What's going on Dad?"

"Where do I start son?" I said with a sigh before trying to start at the very beginning.

After a few minutes I noticed Robbie looked as baffled as I did.

"I know, Robbie, it doesn't make sense does it?"

"No it doesn't dad." Before he could say anything more, two familiar faces appeared at the other end of the garden; it was my aunty and uncle, they often popped round to say hi.

"What's up with Kim?" they said in unison as they approached. They'd obviously encountered her less than charming self when they came in the house. And so I began to retell the story again, with my audience of three all shaking their heads in disbelief.

Suddenly my auntie turned and walked purposefully back up the garden and into the house.

With the back doors open we heard every single word as she calmly and politely asked Kim to explain what was going on in her head, and as Kim ferociously exploded into a torrent of abuse in reply.

"See, this is what I have to put up with on a daily basis," I said to my uncle and Robbie, who flinched in symmetry as another scream erupted from the back door.

I was glad my family had seen it first hand, glad that they knew what I'd been contending with. And losing control so openly seemed to make Kim rethink her ways a little. Over the next few weeks we started to get our relationship back on track; I realised that I wanted it to work because of Joe but also because I still loved her. In our good times she was still my sweet, sweet, Kim.

But in the bad times, she felt like my arch enemy. And Kim's friends weren't helping matters. I knew now that they were capable of closing ranks to hide each other's little secrets and their constant hush-hush meetings made me more than slightly paranoid that there was a secret that I wasn't privy to. I felt uncomfortable in my own home whenever they were around; an outsider to the conversations and whispers that took place right in front of me.

We struggled through the rest of the year, passing through Christmas with a strained happiness and a hollow in my heart. But with the New Year I felt society's pull to make changes.

"Kim, you know I've been working flat out to support you and Joe, but we're really not making ends meet." Kim frowned at me. "I think you should look into getting a job now Joe's that much older," I finished.

Kim just shrugged.

"I need your help Kim, the bills are piling up; you know I wouldn't ask otherwise." I sensed Kim wasn't impressed by my request, and the look on her face almost implied I was saying it to spite her. I didn't back down though, "I've been asking around and there's a nail parlour in Lichfield that would take you on and train you up." Kim seemed shocked that I'd made such progress but it needed to be done. "The guy who owns it is from Vietnam and most of his staff are from Thailand, it'll be perfect for you." I said in my most enthusiastic voice.

Kim's jaw tightened, "I can find my own work Sean," she hissed.

"I know Kim, but we need the money and this is a good job, you'll learn a trade, there'll be people you can talk to and the man seems very nice, he'll look after you..."

She huffed, "Oh ok, if you say so."

The following Saturday I took Kim to the shop in Lichfield and to my surprise she walked in without any fuss.

"Joe and I will pick you up later," I said bending down to kiss her on the cheek.

She glared at me. Not wanting to cause a scene I just smiled and walked out,

"See you at three," I sung as I left the reception area.

Joe and I wandered round the shops while we waited for Kim to finish her first day; it was 2:30 when we enthusiastically went back to the shop. I was excited to see how she was getting on; how her first day was going; I wanted to see her in action. But when we walked into the shop Kim was nowhere to be found.

"Where's Kim?"

I asked the manager, assuming she was out the back or having a break.

"She left at about eleven," he replied.

"Eleven? But why?"

"I don't think she liked the smell of the place," he replied honestly.

Admittedly the fumes were a bit overwhelming, but all the other girls seemed to have gotten used to them, I thought looking along the row of manicure chairs at them all busily working away.

"Err, ok, thanks," I said, slightly embarrassed that I didn't even know where my own wife was. Why hasn't she called me? I thought as I made my way back to the car. I dialled her number on my mobile; it rang and rang.

"Kim, can you call me when you get this message, thanks love."

I tried again.

"Kim, I'm a bit worried about you, where are you. Call me please."

I strapped Joe into the car. One more try, I thought to myself.

"Kim, please, I'm worried now; can you call me as soon as you can, just let me know you're safe."

I drove home, the car's ticking indicator the only sound to interrupt my panicked silence.

I pulled up outside the house, turned the key in the front door, and walked in. I froze in the hallway; I could hear a noise in the living room. I ran in; Kim was laid out on the sofa watching television, without a care in the world.

"Where have you been?" I said, still frantic with worry.

"I didn't like the smell," she said flippantly.

"So why didn't you call me? I would have picked you up, I've been worried to death." I hesitated as it dawned on me what I was worried of.

"Kim, I was scared you'd left us," I revealed emotionally.

I was hoping for an outburst of apology or a declaration of commitment, to Joe if not for me but, heartless as ever, Kim just looked through me. My marriage had become a constant cycle of strops, silence and chilling looks.

Chapter 10 – Visa of love

Weeks passed by and my marriage felt more like the parenting of an angst ridden teenager. Kim was going out most nights, getting drunk, providing very little, if any information about where she was going, who with or if and when she'd return. I felt like a mug. I knew onlookers saw me as one but I always held on to a glimmer of hope that things would turn around, that we could be the family I wanted us to be.

Kim did eventually get a job at the local Thai restaurant, but rather than contributing towards the bills as I'd hoped, all of her wages and tips were spent on her. I despaired, but despairing didn't get me anywhere, nor did arguing, reasoning, or pleading. Kim was a law unto herself. Her selfishness shocked me on a daily basis but in March of that year it reached a pinnacle.

"Sean, you need to give me some money to pay for my visa."

"Kim, I've told you a thousand times, I haven't got any money."

"But I need it. Without it I'm not a full British citizen. I want to be British like you Sean!"

"I know you do, but It's over a thousand pounds, I haven't got that kind of money spare," I felt the epitome of a broken record as I spoke.

"Well find it!" she shouted.

Enough was enough.

"Kim, I've done everything I can for you. You knew this was coming up, why didn't you save any of your earnings?" I asked quite logically. I didn't expect an answer so I continued, "I pay for everything, the house, the bills, the shopping, Joe's clothes, not to mention the loan I took out on the land *you* wanted. I'm not a money tree Kim."

Before I knew it Kim was on her mobile ranting down the phone to her friends; it was all in Thai but I didn't need to speak the language to know that she was berating me with a passion that she savoured specifically for arguments like this one that evolved around money.

Every so often she would say some words in English just to make sure I understood.

"Horrible man... nasty... selfish."

I walked out, unable to listen to another second of her unfounded abuse.

I jumped in the car and found myself driving towards my solicitor's office. Sat in the car park outside I contemplated what I was about to do. I had no alternative.

"I want to get a divorce," I said, surprising myself with the ease at which the words fell from my lips. "And if I can, I want custody of my son. I have to look after him and at the moment I have no idea what she's doing with him during the day while I'm at work."

"Let's start from the beginning," she said calmly, her shiny fountain pen poised ready to jot down notes.

And so I did, starting at the beginning and finishing at the point I got in the car to drive to her office. When I finished she placed her pen slowly on the table, sat back in her high backed leather chair, clasped her hands together and gave me a sympathetic look. I was used to that look; I got it a lot when people learnt the nightmare of my marriage.

"Leave it with me," she said standing to shake my hand.

And as I walked out of her office I felt a sense of relief. I knew I'd finally made a step in the right direction.

Back home, I explained to Kim where I'd been and what I'd done.

Her volcanic temper erupted once again, "You want a fight?" she said, "I'll give you a fight and you will lose!"

I'd lost all my fighting energy, and for once I was the one left staring blankly at my opponent. I was so very tired; I just wanted her out of my life and for Joe to be happy and shielded from all the arguments.

A few days later I had a call from my solicitor; that's quick, I thought as I saw her number flash up on the screen of my phone.

"Don't tell me it's sorted already."

"No, not quite," she laughed. "I'm just calling to ask if you could pop your passport in to my office at some point."

"Err yep, I'll have a look for it but I've got a feeling Kim's got it stashed away somewhere; I'll call you back," I said, hanging up the phone in a fluster. It had suddenly occurred to me that Kim had our passports locked away in a suitcase upstairs; she stowed it under the bed, and had always refused me access to it. What else had she got in there, I thought as I pulled it out from beneath the bed and fumbled with the dials of the combination lock.

"Come on, come on," I said out loud as I tried all of the obvious number combinations I could think of. Perhaps this suitcase holds the key to all the secrecy I thought; and then I stopped still. I felt the colour fall from my face and land in a heavy ball in the pit of my stomach. I pushed the locked suitcase away, sat back on the floor and picked my phone up once again.

"It's me again," I said, "I've got a feeling Kim's planning to do something stupid...with Joe, I mean."

"Ok, don't panic," my solicitor replied, knowing exactly what I was implying. "From now on you need to write things down, everything that she does and says, write it down and bring it to my office every day. I'll notify the passport office, so there's no way she can take Joe out of the country."

Relief was an understatement; even if she did have a plot brewing in that suitcase I'd stopped it progressing, and with that I stood up and kicked the case back under the bed.

But my solicitor still needed my passport.

"Kim, do you know where my passport is?" I said nonchalantly that evening.

"No."

"Kim, I know you do, I need it; my solicitor needs it."

She looked at me with the now familiar hate filled eyes.

"Come on Kim, please, can we be grown up about this, for Joe's sake?"

"My friend has it," she replied, clearly lying, "I'll get it when I'm ready."

My blood was boiling, why was she being so awkward; what was she hoping to achieve?

I marched out of the house and straight to the police station.

"I'm sorry sir, but if you know where it is then it's not really theft and there's nothing I can do." The young PC on the front desk said flippantly.

"You are joking? She's going to kidnap my son!" That was the first time I'd said the words out loud and they instantly caused my voice to crack as I tried to continue pleading. "I know she will. I'm sorry it's just... I'd do anything..." The unsympathetic look in his eyes told me there was no point continuing. I blinked back the tears and walked out of the station.

Why isn't anybody taking me seriously? I thought, as I pulled my car door shut. Why is no one bothered?

Back home I explained to Kim where I'd been and she finally took me seriously, and told me where I would find my passport. At last a breakthrough, I thought, she can be reasonable after all.

The week continued uneventfully, every morning I was faced with the same hostility over the breakfast table and every evening I came home to a house full of Thai people all whispering and laughing, about me or at me I wasn't quite sure, but I didn't like it one bit. It was a Friday evening when I came home to find a fancy BMW 4x4 parked outside the house; with a sleek black paint job, shiny alloys and blacked out windows it was a car that turned heads, but I couldn't think which one of Kim's friends would be the owner of such a beast. None of her restaurant pals were earning enough to afford one of those. I walked in the house intrigued, and found Kim talking to a young Thai girl and a big Italian looking guy. I didn't recognise either of them.

"This is my cousin, from London," Kim said introducing the girl to me. I'd never heard Kim mention a cousin in London. "And this is her boyfriend, Marco," she continued as his outstretched hand thrust itself in my direction.

The four of us went through into the living room, I scooped Joe onto my lap; the atmosphere felt tense, I sensed more secrets were brewing but I just couldn't put my finger on it. Then Kim's cousin said something that made me flinch;

"Are you coming to stay with me Joe?"

"What's going on?" I ordered, "Joe's not going anywhere!"

88

The room went ghostly silent. I exchanged eye contact with each of them before picking Joe up and carrying him into the kitchen, "Let's go and make daddy a cup of tea," I said.

The kettle had barely come to the boil when our guests appeared in the kitchen doorway to say their goodbyes. As the front door shut behind them I called Kim into the kitchen.

"I'm telling you now, I don't know what's going on in your head, but you are not taking Joe anywhere. This is his home!" I slammed the teaspoon on the kitchen side frustrated that I even had to spell it out at all.

"You wanted a fight, so you're going to have one," she said with a smirk.

I could hardly breathe with the emotion that was surging through my body.

The next morning I wrote down the events of the previous day, even down to the last detail of Marco's car, something just didn't add up, and I posted my notes through my solicitor's door on the way to work. Back home that evening there was an unnerving normality in the house; I played with Joe, put him to bed and then Kim sat with me in the living room watching TV; we even shared a joke or two. Where has all this paranoia come from? I thought to myself as I reassessed the events of the last few months. Here we were now being civil, sharing Joe, everything seems normal, I thought, and I went to bed that evening feeling a sense of peace I hadn't felt for a long time.

The next morning I bounced out of bed, kissed Joe goodbye and left the house; I had a long day of work ahead of me and I needed to get an early start. Twelve hours later I returned home to an empty house; I was too tired to analyse it, in fact there wasn't really much to analyse, Kim was often out when I came home, and although I missed Joe, it meant I could spend time without her disapproving stares or snide comments. I took a shower and then went down to the kitchen to grab some dinner. Sitting at the kitchen table I was aware of the wall clock and the second hand ticking resolutely, I looked up, it was nearly nine. She should be home by now, I thought, checking my wrist watch for confirmation.

I flicked through the address book on my phone; Tom, he was a good friend, he'll know what to do, I thought.

"Call the police!" Came his very definite and only instruction.

This can't be happening. We had such a normal day yesterday. The conversation in my head was getting louder and more urgent. She's just trying to scare me... surely.

My next calls were to every one of her friends I could think of. Nobody had seen her, or if they had they weren't letting on. My heart was pounding now, the thought of Joe, gone, snatched away from his familiar surroundings, his toys. His toys, I thought before hurtling upstairs to see if she'd had the consideration to take any of them with her. I flung myself into Joe's bedroom and systematically looked from corner to corner; everything was still in its place; his teddies still propped up at the end of his bed, his toy instruments all spilling out of the toy box under the window. Clothes, I thought, she must've taken some clothes with her. I opened his top drawer, preparing for the worst, but it was still full with his neatly folded shorts and bright t-shirts adorned with various cartoon characters. The second drawer the same; and so it went on. She'd taken nothing. I turned my attention to her room; I scanned the wardrobes, the drawers, everything still in its place.

And then my pulse went on standby as I crouched down to check under the bed. In a split second my heart began to beat again as I saw the suitcase was still there, in its not so discreet hiding place. She can't have gone, not properly, I concluded.

I woke early the next morning and flicked on the news,

"It's the 27th march 2010 and here are the stories for the day," the cheery newsreader said.

I watched, distracted, as I ate my breakfast, half expecting a breakthrough story about a Thai woman being stopped at the airport with her young son. But the story didn't come. At 9am I called my solicitor's office. She was in a meeting. How could she be in a meeting when I need her? I thought, feeling tense once again.

"Well I need to speak to her urgently," I barked at her assistant on the other end of the line, "I need to know if I should call the police, please, please get her to call me urgently," I said breaking down in tears before I hung up the phone.

This was becoming all too real; I'd imagined she'd been planning something, and I'd half let myself think it was possible but I never dreamt it would actually happen, and I'd never realised how painful this moment would feel. Something had been wrenched from my soul, and the adrenalin, fear and hope that palpated in my body was making me feel sick. It was 5pm before my solicitor returned my call.

"She's taken Joe!"

"Listen, please don't worry, she won't get far remember, I've written to the ports, she can't leave the country."

I'd known this all along but the panic had numbed all vital pieces of information in my head.

"Right, yes, of course," I stammered, "So, do I call the police?"

Her answer was a definite yes.

But as I came off the phone I made a conscious effort to calm myself down; my solicitor was right, she'd got no spare clothes with her, she couldn't leave the country, she'd surely be back within a few hours. I decided to leave the police station and just continued ringing every acquaintance Kim had ever laid eyes on. Staring at my phone in between calls, willing her to ring me to let me know they were both safe.

It was 8.30am on the 28th March when I finally walked into the local police station ready to declare my son missing. It had been 2 days since I'd last seen him or heard from her. I started to explain my story to the woman at the front desk but she stopped me halfway through and asked me to take a seat. Perhaps she knew something, I thought as I nervously sat back down in the waiting area. Within minutes a more senior police officer called my name, and directed me to a side room along the main corridor. Oh god, this is going to be bad news, I know it, I thought to myself.

"Mr Felton, we know where your wife and son are," she said with a serious tone.

I breathed a much needed sigh, "Well that's fabulous!" I said before instantly sensing that the lady officer opposite me didn't quite agree with my observation. "Are they ok?" I asked anxiously.

"Mr Felton, your wife came in to see us on the 25th March to inform us that you were abusing her, so she is stopping at a friend's house and we will be coming to see you shortly."

I couldn't believe what she was saying, "But I'm getting a divorce from her, she's the one who's abusive, she doesn't look after our son properly at all!"

Flabbergasted was the adjective of the moment. "I have a solicitor, with a long record of everything that's happened..."

"Mr Felton, please, go home now; an officer will be round to see you shortly."

I couldn't believe how cold she was; I walked out of the station pierced with confusion and loss. Kim had turned my world upside down. I turned the key in the car ignition and drove on autopilot towards my house; staring blankly at the road ahead I hoped I'd catch a glimpse of Joe on the street or in the back of a car. My phone rang; I quickly pulled over to the side of the road.

"Hello."

"Mr Felton, this is Sergeant Harrow, you were just talking to me at the station," the female voice said.

"Yes; what's happened?"

"Mr Felton, I'm calling to tell you there's a missing persons alert for your wife and son."

I instantly began to sob. "But, I've just seen you; you told me you knew where they were?" I couldn't take it all in, "What's going on?" I cried.

"I'm sorry about this Mr Felton but if you could give me all the addresses you have of Kim's friends and then someone will be round to see you."

I duly relayed all of the addresses and numbers that I'd been trying myself over the last couple of days and then drove home in shock. As soon as I shut my front door my home phone rang.

"Mr Felton, we need you to come down to the station immediately."

Well at least they're taking this seriously I thought, as I rushed back out of the house to reverse the journey I'd just made.

I spent two hours at the station, retelling my story, trying to fill in any gaps, spot new clues. And then the officers I'd been dealing with came back with me to my house. I could tell they were expecting something dire, squalid living conditions that would force a woman to run away leaving all her worldly goods behind. But the wide eyes and open mouths said it all, our home was immaculate. I looked at the two women stood admiring my living room, "You have to help me; she'll do something stupid to Joe, I know she will." It pained me to think about it but I had to make them understand exactly what they were dealing with.

And with a nod and a knowing and sympathetic smile they both began searching the house. They went through every pocket of every room, including the loft and the sheds;

"What are you doing? I haven't killed her; what are you looking for. We need to find them, my son is in danger!" I said frustrated by their pointless rifling through my paperwork. I started to cry once more, my whole body was shaking. "Please...help me find him," I wept.

"We're doing all we can Mr Felton," one of the officers said making a feeble attempt to clear up my desk.

"We'll be in touch," the other said, fixing her hat back on her head.

I shut the front door and slumped down behind it, all of my energy had drained from my legs; I felt broken. My phone started to ring in my pocket; I could barely speak through my tears as I answered.

"Dad? Is that you?" It was Robbie. I hadn't told him or my parents what had been going on, I'd been trying to protect them; I didn't want them to feel the pain I was feeling. But I couldn't hide it any longer, and I

94

couldn't explain either, I just cried and wailed until my mobile was wet with tears.

"Dad, I'm coming round, don't move," he said.

Robbie and my parents were at my front door in no time at all, and in that time I still hadn't been able to stop crying; hadn't been able to focus on anything other than the gaping ache in my heart.

The rest of the evening was a blur; my mind trying desperately to sense where my son was; surely the bond between us would allow me to do that, I hoped. Robbie stayed with me, plying me with cups of tea and the sincerest optimism. And at 10:30 I had another call from the police.

"I'm just letting you know that your wife definitely hasn't left any of the ports," the office said.

And in that moment the bond with Joe clicked in, and I sensed him, "Please listen to me," I cried down the receiver, "My son is in Thailand; please, I beg you, just find him."

Chapter 11 – Isolation

I don't know how my mind allowed me to sleep that night but the next morning I woke up with a yearning desire for it to all have been a terrible nightmare. I looked down; I was fully clothed; I remembered how I'd cried myself to sleep. I sat on the edge of the bed and looked across to the mirror. The last three days had taken their toll, my eyes were red and puffy, my face looked drawn, and now I had to brace myself to face another day of anguish. I reached across to my mobile on the bedside table. Looking down at the screen, the voicemail sign was flashing at me; perhaps they've found him, I prayed.

I pushed down the button and trembling I held the phone to my ear.

The unmistakeable cackle that came scorching through my ear left me stunned.

Kim was laughing at me, hysterically laughing down the phone.

"Me and Joe are in Thailand, Seany, speak to you soon!" she sang out before bursting into laughter again.

I felt sick.

"Are you ok dad?" Robbie had walked in halfway through and could see I clearly wasn't; it pained me to listen again but I needed Robbie to hear it too. I played it once more, out loud. There were no words between us, and in our moment of horror I felt helpless.

The police came round later that morning to proudly announce that Kim and Joe were in Thailand.

"I know," I said, "I told you that, and listen to this," I said forcing myself to relive her torturous voicemail once more. "I told you all this was going to happen, why won't anyone help me? Joe is in danger!"

"You don't know that," the two officers said simultaneously, clearly focusing on calming me down rather than facing the facts.

"I do, I know this woman, remember?"

I walked upstairs leaving Robbie to see the officers out. Well that's it then, I thought, I know the score; abduction's not a crime in Thailand and our laws count for nothing over there. My son had gone and I'd never get him back. All the kind words, promises and pointless cups of tea in the world wouldn't get him back. I knew the truth.

Weeks passed by and I was no closer to finding him and that sickly truth that I hadn't wanted to consider, was becoming more of a reality with each second. The truth was; if he was still alive, they'd be getting him ready to sell to someone, my eyes pinched shut to try to stop my brain from thinking it; he'd be sold into the sex trade. I was in so much pain already but the thought of Joe suffering, my beautiful smiling little baby; it took my breath away. I couldn't bear to think of my cheery, laughing little man, feeling scared, or lonely, or in pain. I thought I would die there and then as the misery consumed me.

Days passed by with me on autopilot fielding sympathetic phone calls and trying to continue with the basics; eating, sleeping; but none of it seemed relevant. Each morning I woke up from a disjointed night's sleep, I'd walk downstairs and find the silence eerie; no toys playing a rotation of tinkling nursery rhymes, no laughter from my little boy, the laugh that ordinarily filled every cavity in the house. My house that was now empty, of love, of him.

I got to the bottom of the stairs and collapsed on the floor I couldn't breathe, I was shaking all over, my brain was screaming at me to visualise every single one of my memories of Joe, from the day he was born, his first smile, his first steps. The memories were devastatingly wonderful but I just couldn't cope with them. I tried to pick myself up from the floor to walk out into the garden to escape the visions. But I couldn't find the strength; instead I crumbled on my hands and knees and stayed there weeping, until I could find my breath and clear my head, temporarily at least.

That day was a painful one; I couldn't leave the house just in case I got a call and more importantly because I was comforted by being close to Joe's things. But being there was the epitome of rubbing salt in the wounds. It stung like hell. And then at 3pm my very own salt shaker called again.

"What are you doing, where is Joe, what have you done to him?" I couldn't stop, I needed answers.

"He's safe," Kim said calmly.

"What are you playing at?"

"I want my British citizenship in the UK, I have worked hard and I want it," the evil in her voice left me cold; how could she be talking about papers when she'd just abducted my son.

"If you or your family lay one finger on Joe; I *will* kill you, I'll come to Thailand and search you down, if it takes me my entire life I will do it, I promise you that. And don't even think of selling him or hurting him." I needed to make the most of the opportunity to speak to her so I kept on, "You need help, do you know what you're doing? He is only a baby for god sake!" She put the phone down.

I immediately rang the police again,

"Please help me," I begged, "You have to help me, she's going to kill him, I know it."

"Mr Felton, please listen," the male officer said with a hint of exasperation, "The only way you're going to see your son is if you calm down. If she calls again, be nice to her, tell her you're sorry for shouting at her, tell her she was right for taking Joe, and you were wrong for not getting her the papers to stay in the UK. As far as I can see, you need to get her back in this country and that's the only way you'll see your son again." I didn't like the idea of giving into her, even if it was false but I was willing to give anything a chance. "If she gets into the airport we will arrest her and you can have your son back, OK?" He finished.

I managed to mutter my agreement before hanging up the phone in despair.

I sat down on the sofa, distraught that nobody was prepared to help me. I buried my face into my cupped hands; why doesn't anyone understand what danger he's in, I thought. "It's no good," I said out loud. And at that moment I decided that the only way I would get Joe back was if I did it myself. No matter what it took.

Chapter 12 – Prisoner of War

The next morning I started making plans, but as the news report in the background was painfully reminding me, it wasn't going to be easy to get to Thailand. A volcanic ash cloud had pretty much grounded all flights trying to get out of the UK. Someone up there is testing me I thought, as a silently cursed whoever or whatever was conspiring against me.

So instead I decided to do what Kim wanted, and I asked her to send the visa papers over so that I could get things moving. And with me showing willing, so was she; she let me have her number so I could call her when I needed to, although whether she answered or not was a bit of a lottery. I tried to call her every day and cautiously tried to extract snippets of information that could help me track her down once I finally had the chance to make it to Thailand.

It was a Thursday morning and I hadn't heard from her for two days, I was getting worried. I've got to try one more time, I thought, staring at the telephone number that I now knew by heart. It rang and rang, but just as I was about to give up hope;

"Yes."

"It's me, Sean"

"Yes."

"How's Joe doing?"

"He's fine."

"I haven't heard from you, it's been two days Kim," I said angered that she could be so calm.

"I've been busy."

"Doing what? Where's Joe?"

"He's sleeping. I'm glad you rang Sean," she continued skipping over any conversation related to Joe.

This is Jobe Felton just a few months ago, he was abducted out of
the country on the 26th March 2010, we need all the help we can
get to get him back in the country.

This picture was sent to me only last week the 22nd April, as you
can see in the picture he is distressed and scared, if you think you
can help us please contact the numbers on the back,
all information will be confidential. Thank you for reading this
leaflet Sean Felton

"Why's that? Have you finally come to your senses
and you're going to bring him home?" I said sick of her
heartlessness.

"In a way, yes."

"What do you mean?" I replied switching instantly
to a more amicable tone.

"I'll bring Joe back…if you give me thirty thousand pounds."

I looked at the phone in my hand. I couldn't believe what I'd just heard.

"I'm sorry; you're asking me to give you thirty thousand pounds in return for my son that you've abducted?"

Riled didn't even cover it. On top of everything she was now trying to blackmail me. How did I ever fall in love with this woman? I thought with a knot in my stomach.

I wanted to blast a torrent of abuse but I knew that if I lost it, I might lose Joe, for good.

"Let me think about it," I said as sincerely as possible.

Kim had no idea that the police were so heavily involved; I didn't want to start spouting any legal jargon at her in case it scared her off, but I couldn't converse anymore.

"Tell Joe I love him…"

The phone went dead before I could continue.

I let out a mammalian roar that only slightly alleviated the tension that was swelling in my belly; and then I dropped to the floor and cried.

I don't know how long I was laying there but my sorrowful cries were interrupted when the post landed on the doormat. Looking across from my tear stained spot on the carpet I noticed an interesting package amongst the heap of bills. I pulled myself up and walked over to the front door. Bending down slowly I filtered out the package from its mundane surroundings; it was from Thailand.

I ripped open the well travelled envelope and there in front of me was a photograph of my boy. But instead of feeling relief at seeing his face I was winded with shock. I dropped to my knees, gripping the picture tightly with both hands. What the hell has she done to him?

I ran into the other room and pressed redial.

"What the hell have you done to him?" I screamed as soon as she answered; the gloves were off now.

"What?"

"He looks like something you see on the telly, in a war film, held in a prison camp!" I paused as I realised how true my words were and that I was saying them about our son. "Please Kim, I'm begging you, don't hurt him."

"But Sean..."

"Just let me speak to him, I need to know he's ok."

"I told you, he's asleep."

"You can have anything you want, just don't hurt him. I'll come over to Thailand if you want me to; I'll bring you the money and the UK citizenship; anything you want; please let me speak to him," I begged.

The phone went silent. I sobbed harder as I panicked that she'd hung up on me again, and then I heard Kim's voice, muffled, speaking Thai; I tried to make out what she was saying but it was all too faint, and my uncontrollable tear filled gasps concealed the voices even more. And then I heard him; Joe was screaming, crying; I wanted to reach out and pull him through the phone.

"Don't you hurt him!" I yelled, "Oh god please, help him!"

"I'm not speaking to you," was her callous reply before the phone line went dead.

I thought I was going to die there and then; his screams rang in my ears and my eyes widened as I imagined what horror he was going through.

Suddenly his screams became shriller, what's happening? My confused mind asked. And then I realised that it wasn't his screams, my phone was ringing again.

"Hello," I cried.

"Mr Felton, this is Detective Cooper."

"Please help me," I cried out, "They're going to kill him, you don't know what she's like, she's crazy..."

"Mr Felton, please, calm down..."

"I can't calm down; there's something wrong with her, there must be, she's kidnapped my son!"

"What exactly has happened Mr Felton?"

I couldn't speak anymore, the despair overwhelmed every inch of me.

"Mr Felton, I'm going to call her myself; I'll call you right back."

I just let the phone slip from my hand, convinced it was already too late for Joe.

The next three minutes felt like a lifetime;

"Mr Felton, its Detective Cooper again; I've just spoken to your wife and your son is ok."

I scoffed, "You can't trust her, she's hardly going to tell you anything different is she?"

"Calm down, Sir," he said firmly.

"This is getting me nowhere," I blasted and hung up the phone and quickly dialled Kim's number once more.

Nothing. She'd switched her phone off; I wasn't going to let my frustration get the better of me; I felt more determined than ever that I would do this by myself.

I ran upstairs and pulled out all of Kim's paperwork that she'd left neatly in her top drawer by the side of the bed. I'd been through it a hundred times already but I hoped that I could focus the energy from my new found desperation and find something valuable amongst the pages of notes, scribbles and numbers. As I scoured through the papers I spotted a phone number that I didn't recall seeing before. It was written in faint pencil down one side of a menu from the restaurant where she'd worked. I exhaled a loud breath. Maybe this could be the key I thought, instantly questioning who I would find at the other end of the line once I'd dialled. Come on Sean, pull yourself together I thought as I tried to compose myself to make the first call.

It was a Thai girl who answered; she pretended not to understand me but I knew she did.

"We don't know who Kim is," she said in her most broken English whilst chattering frantically in Thai to another woman who I could hear in the background.

"Please, my son is in danger; he's in real danger, I'm begging you."

The phone went dead.

"Not again!" I roared as I flung my phone across the room.

The tears were streaming down my face uncontrollably, how could anyone be protecting her when a little boy's life was at stake. It was making me question whether society had lost the ability to feel compassion.

Later that evening I tried to call her mum and sister, I knew they didn't speak English but I also knew that if I could just get in touch with them there was a small chance that they could understand the basics of what I was saying. This has got to be my last hope I thought as I carefully dialled the number. I closed my eyes slowly as I listened to the recorded message telling me that their number was unavailable.

I've got to take this higher I decided resolutely. I knew parliament was closed because they where selecting a new government, but there was nothing stopping me contacting the local council and the next day I gave them a call; finally I felt like I was getting somewhere. I had a long discussion with a young girl who gave me the telephone number for a charity called reunite; she told me that they specialised in child abduction cases. I hated hearing the words said out loud. I knew Joe had been abducted but the facts didn't make it easy to hear when the term was banded about so freely. Nervously I dialled the charity's number and proceeded to tell them everything; they sounded hopeful in reply; I felt confident having spoken to them, they were the experts in these cases after all and they pointed me in the direction of the abduction team at the commonwealth office in London.

Once again I recited my story, which was now coming quite naturally, reeling off the facts, and holding back the emotions which sometimes hindered my ability to tell it all exactly how it was; my built in shock absorber often blocking out the most painful details and horrific fears, whenever I had to face them.

"You do know that Thailand is a non Hague country, don't you Sean," the man on the other end of the phone spoke gently, as if it would soften the blow of his words.

"Yes, I know," I said feeling as though I was about to get another door slammed in my face, "But I'm telling you my son is in danger, you need to check on him."

"We can't do that I'm afraid."

"What do you mean? We have police in Thailand I know we do, we need to see if he is safe," I urged. "We can't just do that, I'm sorry."

I listened in disbelief as he went on to explain that they couldn't do anything without Kim's permission.

The person who was most likely to cause him harm was the person who they had to ask if they could check his welfare.

I was losing, whichever way I turned I was faced with obstacle after obstacle that I just couldn't seem to defeat. Red tape, aeroplanes, parliament, everything that could have been put in my path was, and I wasn't sure how much more I could take.

They wound up the phone call, asking for any contact numbers that I had for Kim and her family, but I knew it was more out of courtesy than a desire to do anything with them.

I felt as empty as I had ever felt in my life. I was physically and emotionally drained. I felt as though I was commencing a mourning process for Joe, as the hope of seeing him again dwindled with each second that ticked by. As days passed I didn't know if he was alive or dead, Kim stopped answering her phone all together. My heart, mind and body were numb.

Chapter 13 – Mystic Hope

With every corner of my house unsuccessfully searched for clues to Joe's whereabouts, I felt totally out of my depth; I decided I needed a pro. And I started my hunt on the internet. As I waited for my computer to come to life I shook my head in dismay. I couldn't believe I was actually about to type the words *Private Detective*. As I scrolled down the long list of detectives in Thailand, my cynicism about the country kept pestering my mind. Each name I looked at, and each face I clicked on made me feel uneasy; I couldn't trust anyone. If my own wife could turn against me just to get a bit of cash then a private detective could quite easily just take my money and run, why would they care about Joe's safety, I thought to myself. But then one name kept coming up in my searches, a name that my eye just kept getting drawn to, someone that my gut just told me might be able to help; Gordon Fisk. Having already sent out hundreds of emails to the names I'd found, something made me just pick up the phone and call this one.

"Hello, Gordon Fisk," came the efficient voice.

"Oh hello, my name's Sean Felton; I'm looking for someone to help me find my son."

"Well you've called the right number, can I take a few details."

Gordon was an English chap who, as we spoke, I became assured by. I trusted him, he sounded professional and he sounded optimistic, a feeling that was rapidly dwindling from my own self. We agreed a price and he arranged to send his people out to check an address that I'd obtained. "Please don't give anything away," I said desperately, "If they know I'm on their track they'll run," I finished, now panicking that Gordon could potentially ruin the only lead I had.

"Don't worry, Sean, we know what we're doing. My people will just go around the village selling produce to the local people, nobody will suspect a thing.

I waited patiently for two days; every time I closed my eyes I imagined one of Gordon's men walking through the village and spotting Joe; I imagined the conversation I would have with Gordon afterwards. The joy I would feel knowing his exact whereabouts and that he was safe. As I sat daydreaming about an imminent reunion my phone vibrated in my pocket; I looked down at the screen, I was receiving a picture message. Oh god, I thought, it's going to be a picture of Joe; then I panicked, would he be beaten or hurt?

"Come on!" I yelled at the screen, as the image slowly appeared.

When it did, my heart sank. It wasn't a picture of Joe at all but an image of the hut that I'd sent them to. Entirely boarded up and not a single person in sight. I felt as though I'd been punched in the guts. I went on to read a message from Gordon, apologising that they'd drawn a blank; Kim's family home was abandoned and the village was either closing ranks or genuinely unaware of my beautiful Joe. I rang Gordon straight away.

"So what do I do now?"

"To be honest with you, Sean, it's like looking for a needle in a haystack. Thailand is a big place, it's terrible to say it but in Thailand, children can just disappear, that's why all the criminals come here because they know they won't be found," he paused to let me take in what he'd just said. "If she runs out of money she'll call you I'm sure of that, that's all the Thais want money, money and more money."

"But what about Joe?" I said, close to tears again.

"I'm sorry Sean but I can't do anything else at this time, you have no phone numbers and there's nobody at the addresses you've given me. I've got nothing to go off."

I hung up the phone. Gordon Fisk couldn't help me, the private detective with hundreds of solved cases under his belt had come to a blank; it wasn't looking good.

It had been about 9 weeks since I'd seen Joe, since I'd held him in my arms and stroked his beautiful black hair. And from the moment he'd been snatched I realised that my life meant nothing without him. I still felt that the key to getting him back was out there somewhere, and I turned once again to the fountain of all knowledge, the internet. I wasn't quite sure what I needed to search for but as I randomly flitted from one story to another, learning how other parents had struggled, I suddenly recognised a familiar name, Lorraine Butler; she was a local author and a spiritualist medium. I'd read one of her books about a year ago and I'd really connected with it, so much so that at the time I even tried to contact her to discuss it all further. Her ideas, her knowledge and her hopes fascinated me. But every time I'd tried to call she never answered. After some time I just gave up trying and life moved on. But now, sitting at my kitchen table in front of my laptop, my life had well and truly stopped and with this woman's name dominating my screen I felt compelled to try and call her one last time.

This is ridiculous, I thought as I listened to the phone's monotonous ring.

"Hello."

She'd answered. "Err, hello, I read your book last year and really liked it."

"Oh yes."

"Well I was wondering if I could come to see you, it's very important," I said, uncertain whether I was coming across as slightly insane.

"Well yes you can. Hold on," she said, and the phone went silent for a few seconds, "I can see a young lady and a small boy."

I instantly started to cry. "Oh please don't tell me they have gone," I cried.

"No they haven't, they're not in spirit."

I could suddenly breathe again and I arranged to visit her the next day to talk properly. I'd given her no clues as to why I was calling and yet she'd immediately seen Kim and Joe. Maybe this was the breakthrough I needed.

It was a bright Sunday morning, the roads were relatively empty so I arrived at her house earlier than we'd arranged. I sat outside for a while focusing on Joe in the hope that I could convey every element of him to this amazing woman, who just knew. I got out of the car and slowly walked up the uneven path, lined by rose bushes. I rang the bell, stepped back and waited.

"Hello Sean," she said with a broad welcoming smile.

I'd forgotten how to smile that intensely.

We shook hands and she led me through to her front room.

Walking through her house I was fascinated by the pictures and knickknacks that adorned every free inch of wall or surface. Every item seemed to be placed intentionally, as if there was significance in its being there; pictures of cloudless skies, statues of cherubs and china plates with meaningful passages scrawled across them; every item a source of inspiration.

"I'll record everything I say to you then you can take the tape home with you and listen to it, because you will forget what's been said," she said as she fumbled with an old cassette player.

"Oh ok, yes that's fine, thanks," I said nervously.

"Well I know you've been brought here for me to calm you down; your granddad is telling me," she said plainly.

I was dumbfounded. I waited anxiously to see what else she had to say; with the only thing I really wanted to hear being that Joe was safe.

She went on, "You do know that you will see Joe again."

"Really?"

"Oh yes," she said with a kind smile.

We talked some more; although I mostly listened, I didn't want to miss a word.

"Sean, I'm sorry to say this but Kim was only ever after the money, nothing else."

I'd already started to come to terms with that fact but her confirmation helped to cement it in my heart. I nodded acceptingly.

"I can see a lady, in Thailand," she said closing her eyes to concentrate, "She's pointing to a wooden hut, I can see her finger pointed out straight," she said mimicking the vision in her mind.

She couldn't tell me where that hut was but as I left our meeting that morning, tape clutched in my hand, I felt a sense of peace, and was filled with more determination than ever, to find my boy.

Chapter 14 – New Determination

Over the next few weeks I persisted with my search with a new found vigour. A new government was elected in and I felt it was the perfect time to get them involved too so I booked a meeting with my new MP,

Aiden Burley. He hadn't actually got an office and so a meeting was arranged in the local library. I arrived early with a folder full of information and pictures of Joe, and sat tensely at a table and waited. A young lad came over and introduced himself as Mr Burley's assistant.

"Aiden won't be long," he said trying to ease the awkward silence, "He's a very busy man, what with only just winning his position."

I looked into the lad's eyes and found tears began rolling down my face uncontrollably.

"You have to help me," I pleaded, "Nobody will help me; you're my last chance. My son is going to die and nobody gives a shit!"

My heartfelt outburst stunned him, "Err, I'm sure we can help you," he said, trying his best at a reassuring smile.

Aiden came over to the table to find me hurriedly trying to wipe away my tears.

"You must be Mr Felton?" he said, holding out his hand for me to shake, "Please, come in."

I gathered up my things and followed him into his office.

"So, I've read through the document that you emailed to me. You are in touch with REUNITE and the commonwealth office, aren't you?"

"Yes, but they can't help me, that's why I've come to you. You're an MP, I want Westminster to know what's going on, and to help me get my son back," I said confidently.

"I have no contact with him, I don't even know if he's alive."

"I see."

"I know she'll have abandoned him somewhere; he's on his own," I said with that feeling of panic that set in whenever I thought too hard about what was happening to him. "I need you to help me." Aiden just looked at me, rubbed his hand back and forth across the lower part of his face in thought, and then said, "If it was France I would come with you to get your son, but I'm not coming to Thailand, I'm sorry. I will look into it and let you know," he said standing up to signal the end of our meeting.

Disappointment didn't come close to describing how I felt at that moment. In a daze I stood up and shook his outstretched hand.

"Good luck and keep your chin up," he said dismissively.

I walked out of that library sobbing like a baby. I didn't care who saw me, or what anyone might have thought. By the time I reached home I'd run out of tears but my heart still ached.

Mum called me as I soon as I walked through my front door.

"Well?" she said eagerly, expecting me to announce a national campaign and Downing Street involvement.

"He couldn't help; he's going to look into it."

We both cried together.

With parliament unable to help I knew that the next most powerful force was the media. I started with my local paper, the *Chase Post*. I was put through to Mike, the editor, and pleaded for his help. He didn't need convincing and he arranged for a reporter to come round that day.

Jan came to my house with a small Dictaphone, an A5 notepad and a sympathetic ear. She sat attentively scribbling down notes and occasionally asking questions, but mostly she just listened while I explained the whole story. The tears fell as they did now on a daily basis, and I could tell that Jan was struggling not to do the same.

"Please can you help me?" I said taking a deep breath, having reached the end of my tale and the end of the line as far as my search was concerned.

"We'll do all we can," she said with a delicate smile.

That Thursday, the *Chase Post* dropped onto my doormat. I picked it up and read my story just as Jan had heard it. As I read the first phone call came, it was an old friend from school, he wanted to wish me well, and then another, an old colleague, sending positive thoughts. The phone rang all day, with seemingly my entire local community wishing me the best, and praying that I would bring Joe home safely. Their positivity lifted my spirits and reenergised me for my continued quest.

I spent the next few weeks talking to other papers, calling more potential but unfruitful leads in Thailand, and trying to keep my head above water. It was a Tuesday morning, and I was preparing myself for another stressful day battling with the Thai authorities. I switched on the television to see an almost familiar scene. It was Bangkok, but it looked like a warzone. The red shirts were fighting; the sea of red running wild through the streets with the government's army countering their attacks left me in a cold sweat. What if Joe's in the middle of all that, I feared. I grabbed my phone and rang the police, the images still playing out on my TV. I begged them to do everything they could to get Joe out of there but they insisted that he wasn't in the danger zone. I rang the commonwealth office to confirm what the police were telling me, but it still didn't sit well with me. If they knew for certain that he wasn't there why couldn't they just find him? I made a

115

point of calling the police and the commonwealth office every day from then on. I knew they couldn't help me but I didn't want them to forget me, or more importantly, forget about Joe.

My search was proving hopeless. I needed to take my story higher; further, so I started to call some of the bigger newspapers. I thought they'd snatch up the chance to tell my story but apparently until Joe and I were reunited, there wasn't a full story to run.

"But that doesn't make sense," I said, baffled by what I was hearing, "How can I be reunited if I don't know where he is? I need you to help me find him."

"I'm sorry sir; by all means get in touch once you've found him."

"Have you any idea of the danger Joe is in?"

"I can understand you're upset sir but I'm afraid we simply can't run half a story, I'm sorry."

Wow, I thought as I hung the phone up. What a kick in the teeth. My loss, my heartache and my desperation, wasn't enough for them; it was half a story yes, because in losing Joe I'd lost half of me.

Thankfully the fighting in Bangkok had come to an end and things over there were looking a lot calmer; one Saturday morning I sat out in my garden, remembering how Joe used to play so happily with his football or with me pushing him along on his ride-on toy. I could feel his pain, his fear; if I could die for him I would, I thought to myself, and then I prayed out loud and through wails of tormented emotion, "...Please God, I just want him to be safe...Please," I finished.

I walked back into the house, needing to be away from the garden where Joe had spent so many happy days; back indoors I still couldn't curb my tears, even

116

when a knock on the door momentarily stopped my sobs.

It was my pal, Tom.

"Alright?" he said, clearly observing that I wasn't, "I've just come to check on you."

"I'm sorry Tom, I didn't know anyone was coming round," I said still weeping.

He reached out and put his arms around me. "It'll be ok, you just have to fight," he said encouragingly. "If no one will help, you just have to fight."

Something triggered me to take in what he was saying and after he'd left I looked at myself in the mirror. I looked at the weary man, eyes dark with worry, brow permanently furrowed, channels practically worn into my cheeks where my tears had run so freely, every day for months. That's it, I resolved; I'm not going to cry again; people will listen to me and I will find Joe, even if it's the last thing I do.

The following Monday I proceeded to call every one as normal, the police, the commonwealth office, the press; but this time I wasn't upset, I listened to their negative replies, them saying they couldn't help, and instead of my usual rant of despair I calmly informed each and every one of them that I would get him back and that I would be going to Thailand and bringing him back myself. I told them of my plans to start a campaign, inspired to do so by the inherent wrong in nobody helping when a child's life was in danger. My final call of that morning was to my local MP's office again to arrange a second meeting. I needed to get his support if I was going to battle the Thai government's rules and regulations, which as far as I could tell were only there to make my mission, a true, mission impossible.

Well that was simple enough, I thought as I hung up the phone and finished pencilling our meeting time in the diary; "Ten o'clock tomorrow," I said out loud as I underlined it thoughtfully.

The next morning, as I waited for Aiden Burley to appear, I felt stronger, more determined than ever, and most importantly more confident than ever that I would get Joe back where he belonged.

"Mr Felton, lovely to see you again," Aiden said in a loud voice as he approached.

I stood up to return the greeting.

"This is a friend of mine, Peter; I hope you don't mind, Sean, but I've asked him to sit in with us to see if he can shed any more light on our options," Aiden said ushering for us to shake hands.

"No, not at all, the more people on my side the better," I said positively.

We started the meeting with niceties; tea, and biscuits were circulated around the table and small talk was abundant. But I wasn't there for small talk,

"Mr Burley, I know you're a very busy meeting and I don't want to hold you up any longer than necessary, so if I could just explain the situation as it stands now?"

"Oh, of course, yes Sean, please go on."

"Well, clearly Joe is still somewhere in Thailand, and the longer he's left unfound the greater the risk that something," I swallowed hard, "...well, that something terrible will happen to him."

A moments silence filled the room as we all contemplated what could be.

"Indeed," Mr Burley said, thankfully cracking the silence, "So what have you got in mind?"

"I'm intending to go to Thailand myself; I'm finding Joe on my own."

"Wow, well we'll do whatever we can to support you," he thought for a moment, "I'll start by writing to the embassy in Bangkok and let them know exactly what's happening," he said with a fighting spirit in his voice. "You'll need to take lots of copies of all of your paperwork when you go just in case something happens to you while you're out there."

I hadn't even considered that something might happen to me; all I cared about was that something didn't happen to Joe.

"Yes, of course," I mumbled, suddenly panicking about what could happen.

"I wish you all the best, Sean; I sincerely do." And with that all three of us took to our feet to share an empowered look; it felt as if I was being sent out into battle. A battle I hoped I could win.

Back at home I started to gather up all the paperwork I could find, his advice had been wise, even if it had shaken me slightly. I rummaged through my bedroom collecting photos and notes I'd made over the months; then I noticed a large storage box poking out from under the bed. I stared at it for a moment trying to work out whether I'd opened it recently or even if I could recall what was stored inside. I had no idea; I slowly stood up from my seat and walked over to the side of the bed, knelt down and dragged out the battered box, using both hands to free it from the slats it was rammed against. Opening it up I realised it was stuffed with Kim's belongings, old handbags, scarves, make-up, jewellery. I'm surprised she left that I thought as I picked up a bright rose gold bracelet, and remembered the day I gave it to her. Then something else caught my eye; another scrap of paper with an address written neatly in pencil, in one corner. It was written in Thai but it was definitely an address I hadn't seen before. I squinted to make out the lettering; c h i a n g r a i; 'Chiang Rai?' I queried to myself. I had no idea where that was but something inside told me it was important. I immediately rang the Private Detective who had still been working steadily in the background. I knew he would tell me the truth, "Well Chiang Rai is some distance," he said.

"Just tell me everything you know," I said.

We chatted for about an hour trying to determine the right course of action. We both agreed that this was a lead that definitely felt strong.

"Right, so it's decided then, I won't check out the address straight away; if they get wind that I know where Joe is they'll run, that's a definite. No, I need to play this cool."

I also needed a way to get into Thailand without going through Bangkok airport, and over the next few weeks I worked out every last detail. I planned my way in and my way out, and I prayed that it would be with Joe in tow. As I sat in front of my computer scrolling through my plan once more I noticed a message pop up in my inbox. I didn't recognise the sender. I opened it.

I don't know if this will help but this was Kim's email address when she lived in England...

I was shocked, I didn't even know she had her own email address; I quickly jotted it down into my ever expanding file of notes. I knew there wasn't much point in emailing her; if she wasn't answering my calls she certainly wouldn't take the time to write back to me. So I just held onto it, as I did with every new titbit of information that fell in my path. I kept my solicitor informed of every new development, no matter how big or small, and visiting her office each morning was becoming part of my daily routine. I needed routine, I needed to fill my day with purposeful actions, if I didn't I feared I might just stop, lose momentum; I couldn't let that happen. And so after another long day of phone calls, meetings, research and planning, I wearily climbed into bed. It was eleven pm, a relatively early night based on recent weeks; I always seemed to get engrossed in another clue just before I intended to go to bed and two hours later I'd still be no closer to Joe, but a whole lot more emotionally and physically drained.

As I lay my head back on my pillow I looked up at the ceiling to visualise Joe's face, as I did every night. I wanted to remember his smile, his giggle that made my heart bleed with love. But every now and then the photo that Kim had sent me sneaked into my mind and cruelly tainted all of my happy thoughts. I squeezed my eyes tightly closed and clenched my teeth together to expel the image.

"Damn it!" I said sitting up in anger. At that moment I couldn't have hated Kim more.

I knew I wouldn't get to sleep easily now, I looked around the room wondering what I could do to distract myself. With my eyes landing on my laptop at the end of the room I suddenly had a thought; Facebook. I don't know why I hadn't considered it before now, it was *the* social network, the place where everybody knew everybody and everything. I felt invigorated. I jumped out of bed and switched the laptop on, my fingers poised ready to type her name into the search bar. I carefully typed, Kim Felton, the name that now filled me with emptiness. No search results found. Perhaps she's using her Thai name, I thought quickly; Saowapak Felton, still nothing. Hmmm, maybe she's ditched the Felton all together, I thought. There was a long list of Saowapaks, clearly a common name in her part of the world, just my luck, I huffed, but undeterred

I systematically clicked on each and every one. It wasn't long before a familiar face was there on my screen; it was her, Kim was staring coldly into my eyes, as if she didn't have a care in the world. In a tight cherry red dress, surrounded by men in a typical Thai bar, I'd found Kim.

"I've found her," I shouted hysterically as I began running around the house, "I've found her, I've found her!" I ran to find my mobile, and dialled my mum's number; by the time she'd answered I'd broken out into wild laughter.

"Whatever's going on Sean, do you know what time it is?"

"I've found her mum; I've found her!"

There was no doubt that I sounded like a mad man but I didn't care and I simply couldn't stop. I ran back to the computer once more;

"It's definitely her mum, on Facebook, and it's a recent photo." I slowed down to take in the revelation, "I'm getting closer mum."

My mum just cried.

When I'd finally calmed down I realised the significance of seeing Kim's face jumping out of my screen. I'd been defiantly optimistic up until now, but this gave me actual hope, something that I'd half heartedly convinced myself I'd had but that now I truly felt. I've got to be smart, I thought; this is precious, one wrong move and she'll be gone; Joe will be gone.

Chapter 15 – A Technological Lair

The next morning I called Robbie, "Hello son, I've got some good news, I've found her."

"What? Where? Where's Joe?"

"One step at a time," I said with a chuckle, "I've found her on Facebook, and I need you to come round and help with something."

"Of course, anything, what do you need?"

"I need to set up a false account; I'm going to be the type of person that Kim won't be able to resist talking to."

"Oh you mean rich then?" Robbie said observantly, "I'll be round in a few minutes Dad."

Robbie ran round to my place; he was as desperate as I was to get Joe back.

In front of the computer we sat side by side staring at the woman who had turned our lives upside down.

"Do you know what I have to do?" I asked naively. I'd been on Facebook briefly but I knew Robbie was a whizz at all things technical.

"Yep, not a problem, we just need a name; how about Matt, sounds casual but quite trendy, no?"

"Matt…Young?" I asked.

"Matt Young it is," Robbie clicked away at the keyboard. "Now how about his profile?"

"I want her to think she's talking to a rich businessman type; from the US," I added spontaneously.

Robbie did what he had to do while I sat back in awe and slowly watched Matt Young come to life on the screen. We randomly picked out a profile picture from the internet; a good looking man in his thirties, tanned, well groomed; the perfect decoy. With a bit of refining Robbie made Matt sound genuine, a businessman with an interest in Thailand. We didn't waste any time and immediately hit the button to request Kim as a friend.

"All done," Robbie said, sitting back smugly into the chair.

"So now we've just got to wait for her to take the bait," I said feeling ever closer to my baby.

The next morning I woke up and went straight to the computer, I logged on, my hands trembling as I waited for the page to click in. And then there it was. She'd accepted my friend request. Kim was Matt's friend. Without a second thought I flicked through all of Kim's photos, examining the scenery, the buildings, the road signs, to try and work out exactly where she was in Thailand. There was a common theme in most of the photos, Kim laughing and joking with two white guys; I couldn't work out their relationship or why these guys were in Thailand but I was on a roll so I decided to request their friendship on the site that was now opening up a world of possibilities for me. I hadn't hoped for much but to my absolute shock they not only accepted my friendship but along with Kim, they all started chatting quite openly with Matt Young.

But my curiosity didn't stop there, if Kim was regularly on the internet then she must also be using email again, so I dug out the email address that I'd been sent and carefully compiled an email to send to her, this time from my true identity. Within a day I saw her name appear in my inbox. I felt dread as I hovered the cursor over it; not sure whether opening it would reveal my worst fear, or even any number of my fears, which were all as terrible as the next.

Dear Sean,

Joe is fine. We had a birthday party for him and he had a new bike…

I knew it was all lies; she'd already revealed to Matt young that she'd spent the last eight or nine weeks with her two male friends partying in Thailand. And a children's birthday party certainly wasn't on the agenda. She lied so easily and so frequently and yet it still shocked me. I wasn't used to such deceit coming so freely. Searching through the Facebook photos again I found hundreds of pictures that confirmed what all three were telling Matt Young. The net is closing in, I thought, although I still hadn't seen or heard anything about Joe, nothing concrete anyway.

I decided to feed a small piece of my knowledge into the relevant authorities, namely the commonwealth office and the police. But I didn't let them in on too much. I'd discovered over the last few months that the only person I could trust to get things done properly was me. I told those who asked that I'd tracked her down and we were talking via email. I couldn't risk a pen-pusher behind a desk, quoting red-tape at me and somehow coming in the way of being reunited with Joe; my cards were as close to my chest as they could possibly be.   The email conversations got more and more detailed as the days and weeks went by, with Kim displaying some surprising honesty, a quality I didn't think she was capable of conveying.

You are a nice man, Sean, a good man, she wrote. *You have done nothing wrong; I know that, I just really wanted to be a UK citizen...that is why I took Joe.*

It wasn't news to me but seeing it in black and white, so painfully frank, cut me deeply. I read it over and over again before the emotion flowed, I cried once more, the tears I thought I'd left behind me were back, and all because she'd finally admitted that my son was taken because of her selfishness. I'd read it and now I needed the police to read it. I hit the print button and waited for the printer to go through the motions before it spat out the cruel words. I slowly folded it over picked up my jacket and left for the station; finally things were coming into place.

Back from the station I felt hopeful once more; the police were as shocked as me about her open declaration of guilt and lies. And we all felt that it was only a matter of time before her web collapsed. Let's get back online I thought, pulling up a chair in front of the computer once more. I tapped in the Facebook login details that I'd now memorised I'd used them so frequently. I gnawed nervously on my bottom lip as I realised that neither Kim nor her two friends were online, and that I hadn't heard from any of them for two days. I concocted another leading message that I hoped would encourage a reply. I clicked send and whispered a quiet prayer, questioning why I suddenly had a bad feeling about Matt Young.

The next morning I checked for a reply; it wasn't there. That evening I did the same; nothing. I rested my elbows on my desk and dropped my head into my hands; they're onto me, I thought, I've pushed it too far. I stared at the screen, shaking my head at my incompetence, and then, with nothing left to lose I decided to be brave; I decided to work with the truth. Mum always said honesty's the best policy, I thought as I opened up my own email account and began to write to Kim's two friends. That was one of the hardest emails I'd ever had to write. I wanted them to help me, but I had to word it carefully knowing full well that if it went wrong I wouldn't ever see Joe again. I told them my story, giving as many facts about Kim as I possibly could to help convince them I was telling the truth. I double checked my phone number and pressed send. I'd sealed my fate one way or another.

It was the following day when my phone started ringing in my coat pocket; I fumbled to pull it free, and looked at the screen; withheld.

"Hello."

"Hello, iz zat Sean Felton?" came a strong European accent.

"Yes, who's this?" I said, knowing instantly that it was one of my Facebook acquaintances.

"This is Marcus, you sent me an email?"

In reply I breathed out a sharp mouthful of air; he'd rung.

"Are you still there Sean?"

"Yes, I'm here, I'm sorry, I'm just a bit shocked that you called."

"I had to," he said sensitively. "We checked out your story on the internet, we saw your pictures in the paper, we know that what you are saying iz la truth," he finished, his accent sneaking through.

Marcus went on to explain that he and his friend were both French and they had been travelling in Thailand when they met Kim and started to spend time with her.

"Please, can you tell me, have you seen my son?"

"I am sorry to say this but we have been with Kim for a long, long time and we did not see your son."

My throat, heart and gut sank as low as they could go.

"Kim told us she had a son, but she said she was married to a Thai guy?"

"No, she lied. She's married to me. She lies all the time."

"Yes we've found that out for ourselves; she's told us many stories that just do not..." he paused as he struggled to think of the English translation.

"They don't add up," I said helpfully.

"Definitely not. I'm so sorry my friend; we didn't know she was your wife."

"I know," I replied, "I just need to find Joe."

"We'll do whatever we can to help you Sean."

"Can you speak to her? Get any information you can from her so that I can get Joe back. I need to come over there and bring him back; please, will you help me?"

"Of course, but please; who is Matt Young?"

I didn't want them to know that I'd been as deceitful as Kim, "He's my private Detective," I fibbed.

"Private detective? Wow, you really mean business."

"Yes, I do; everyone's involved in this, the police, the government, they all know about Joe's kidnapping and they're all working to get him back. We need you to help us," I pleaded, trying to convey the significance of their role.

"We will help you, we will, we promise, but can Matt Young be trusted," Marcus asked.

"Oh yes," I smiled to myself, "he's very trustworthy."

I could tell that Marcus and his companion were genuine holidaymakers who had unwittingly gotten involved in my life dramas because of their chance meeting with Kim. But I was hopeful that they would respond to my heartfelt plea and work with me.

Exactly one week later they did.

"Sean, it is Marcus."

"Have you got some news?"

"Yes, we know where your son is; this is his address..."

My hands couldn't move fast enough, I wrote and recited the address three times just to make sure I had it down perfectly.

"My friend, you have to be quick, we know that Kim is planning a trip back there very soon."

"Thank you, thank you, I'll keep in touch," welling up I was overcome by the kindness of two strangers; "I really do appreciate you helping me like this."

"Bonne chance, Sean."

I put the phone down, my mind was leaking information, I didn't know if I could trust these guys but I had to go with it, why would they call back if they didn't want to help me, I thought. I couldn't stop now anyway, I couldn't risk passing up this lifeline. I called the police and told them I knew where Joe was, I listened to my voice saying the words but it still didn't seem real. As soon as I'd finished my call to the police my phone rang, it was REUNITE calling to see if I'd made any progress. They were as shocked as me that I'd got so far on my own, but they advised me that the next step would mean getting a specialist solicitor involved. They knew what they were talking about and I wasn't going to argue so my next call was to a solicitor in Stoke. He had a free appointment for the very next day; although I sensed he may have just picked up on the urgency in my voice and cleared some room in his diary for me; either way, at 10:40 the following morning I found myself sitting in his office admiring the sea of certificates that adorned the walls on either side. Well at least it looks like he knows what he's doing, I thought in awe. We spent one hour exactly discussing next steps; he was very efficient, and knew the bureaucracy that surrounded abduction cases in Thailand. I felt confident that he was absolutely the best man to have on the job.

Back home, with a new found sense of purpose I rang the abduction team at the commonwealth office, and finally announced the news I'd been longing to say,

"I'm travelling to Thailand; I know where my son is so I'm going to get him back; I've been advised that you can contact the British Embassy in Bangkok and let them know my intentions."

I couldn't believe that little old me, Sean Felton, was having dealings with the British Embassy, but the next big step was yet to come. The following Wednesday I found myself navigating through the hectic streets of London, in a daze. I had to appear in the High Court to get a ward of court and full custody of Joe; I knew that this wouldn't mean a thing in Thailand but I needed to be armed with everything I could possibly get my hands on to help convince the Thai authorities that Joe should be with me. It was a relatively straight forward process and after an arduous wait, the following Friday the formal documentation dropped through my letterbox. I felt like I'd struck gold already; someone had finally confirmed that Joe should be at home with me.

Throughout all of my meticulous planning and negotiating I remained in contact with Kim, asking her politely if she would consider letting me see Joe. I didn't let on that I fully intended to see him whether she liked it or not, and she cruelly denied me at every opportunity, satisfyingly unaware that in a matter of days we would be walking on the same soil and she wouldn't have a choice. From the moment I had my hands on the final piece of legal documentation I booked a last minute flight to Thailand, leaving Birmingham the very next day.

I made my friend Tom aware of all my plans, giving him copies of all the papers and important phone numbers, reiterating that there was a high chance that things could go wrong for me; after all, not many people battled the Thai system and won. I didn't share my worries with my parents or Robbie but as they saw me off at the airport I could see in their faces that they had already worked it all out for themselves.

"It'll be fine mum, just you wait and see; next week Joe will be running around your back garden," I said before hugging her tightly. I was saying the words but there was no emotion, I was numb, with fear, with worry and with a hope that I wasn't sure I should be allowing myself to feel.

"Stay safe, son," she whispered.

I walked through into the departure lounge clutching tightly onto my hand luggage which held my destiny, all of the paperwork that would help me get my son back. I went through the security procedures as I'd done many times before and after a long wait I boarded the plane. Settling down in my aisle seat I was very aware that I didn't feel any of the excitement or anticipation that I'd felt on previous trips to Thailand. The monitor in front of me was charting our route but all I could see in my mind was the route back home, hopefully with a special passenger in the seat next to me. I felt angry that I had to be making the trip at all, but this time I meant business. I didn't know what to expect, I didn't know what I was supposed to be feeling and so I just tilted my head back, closed my eyes and dreamt of fatherhood.

After hours of dreaming, praying and hoping we finally landed in Bangkok. The exciting vibe that the airport always previously portrayed left me cold this time, the bright smiles seemed false and the previous paradise promised seemed a million miles away. My paradise now would be snuggled up at home with Joe. I walked solemnly through to collect my luggage, observing all the honeymooners and enthusiastic young men eagerly larking around the airport ready to commence their holiday. I remembered being one of those men, thinking I was about to embark on a dream holiday; I shook my head, remembering that at the time it was a dream holiday and if it wasn't for that trip I wouldn't have had the joy of Joe in my life at all; I couldn't regret it all. The Tannoy system clicked in prior to a woman making a standard announcement in Thai, her voice was like that of an old friend, I'd heard it so many times before, but this time it held no charm, no splendour in the intricate language with its poetic tones. I walked on straight up to the security desk for my photo to be taken, a miserable mug-shot at its best; I had no time for smiles today. Through the imposing glass doors I jumped into a waiting taxi and leant forward to give him the address of the hotel I'd booked into. He scanned it, nodded and then pulled away from the airport.

"So, is this your first time to Thailand?" he asked happily.

"No mate, it's not. I know Thailand very well." He looked into his rear view mirror, searching for more. We made eye contact but that was all he was getting; I wasn't going to risk anything on this trip, my arrival had to be a complete surprise for Kim; I hadn't come this far just for a nosey taxi driver to break my cover. The rest of the journey was awkwardly quiet and it felt longer than the flight from the UK but after travelling through miles of markets, towns, villages and emptiness we finally pulled up at my hotel. It was a quaint affair that I'd found on the internet back home; it was owned by an English guy and importantly it was just minutes away from the British Embassy. I couldn't wait to get to my room, kick off my shoes and relax, it had been a long and stressful journey, and I'd forgotten how imposing the heat was; I was dripping. I jumped in the shower and washed away the journey. Then I lay on my bed to rest; I hadn't intended to but I must have dropped off to sleep instantly and before I knew it I could hear maids outside my room getting ready to start their morning duties. I quickly got dressed in my khaki linen trousers and a cool blue cotton shirt and went downstairs for breakfast. I met several welcoming faces on my way, but each of them just left a bad taste in my mouth, they reminded me of Kim. I settled down at a table before a large white guy came over and introduced himself.

"Good morning, how did you sleep?"

"Oh, yes like a log, thanks."

"I'm Paul, the owner here," the man said offering out his right hand.

"Sean, pleased to meet you," I replied.

"Have you been to Thailand before?"

"Yes a few times," I said, not really wanting to talk about it, so I switched the questions back to him, "What about you? How did you find yourself out here?"

"I've been here for many years," he said, "I've got nothing left in the UK, this is my home now."

We spoke for a few minutes before I disclosed that I needed to get to a meeting at the embassy. I could tell he was curious but I still couldn't let on the true reason for my visit.

"I'll arrange a taxi for you, Sean, leave it with me!"

He walked over to the bar, reached across and grabbed his phone. While he chatted a young waitress brought me some breakfast; a full English, Thai style. I felt famished so I tucked in immediately, barely pausing to say thank you to the young girl smiling politely at the side of my table. Moments later Paul was back, inviting himself to sit down at my table.

"So, you must have been here when all that trouble with the red shirts was going on?" I said, still not wanting to talk about me.

"Oh yes, it was terrible," he replied.

"By the look of things on the news Bangkok was a warzone."

"Oh it wasn't just Bangkok, we had people all over the country trying to flee the troubles," he said.

"Really? I didn't realise."

"Oh yes, Bangkok, Chiang Rai, all over," he finished before taking a swig from a cup of tea.

Chiang Rai; the name instantly sent my mind ringing with alarm bells, that was exactly where Joe was. "Is everything ok now?" I asked cautiously.

"Well it is and it isn't, just keep your eyes open."

I wasn't quite sure what I should be keeping my eyes open for but I nodded in agreement nonetheless, "I will do, thank you."

I finished my breakfast just as the taxi driver called my name. And with paperwork all in order I jumped in the back of his car for another silent journey. I didn't care if I came across as ignorant, I just needed to concentrate on Joe; there was no time for small talk if I was to focus all my energy on finding him.

"This is it!" the driver announced.

I looked out of the passenger window, a very English looking building, I thought as I reached for some cash to pay the driver. And once out of the car I took a deep breath and composed myself before walking towards the security guard.

"I've got an appointment here this morning."

"Name?"

"Sean Felton."

134

"Identification?"

He obviously didn't feel like small talk either, I thought to myself as I opened up my file to present the appropriate letters and certificates.

"This way, please," the man said; his face barely moving.

At the next security gate I had to remove my watch and hand over my phone and money. It all felt very surreal, what on earth did they expect me to do, I thought. Eventually I made it to the main reception area. I handed over my letter to the professional looking woman behind the desk.

"Take a seat please, I'll get someone to see you," she said almost instantly.

I sat down at one end of the long corridor, the only person on the long row of seats propped up against one wall. Without my watch I wasn't exactly sure but it felt like I'd been waiting for about five minutes when another woman bellowed my name into the vacuous corridor. I stood up, almost to attention; the heat had started to get the better of me again and I could feel the back of my shirt was sticking where it once hung freely.

"Come with me," the slim woman announced walking in front of me into a small interview room.

Once inside I handed over all of my files. She neatly shuffled them on her desk before opening up the first document. I gave her a moment to get up to speed before I spoke, "I now know that Kim is working as a prostitute, and she's not with my son anymore, but I do have an address for him; I desperately need to find him," the words didn't come out how I'd rehearsed them but I'd made my point.

"If you could just tell me the whole story Mr Felton," she said kindly.

And so I began. It wasn't long before I saw the glint in her eye slowly dwindle away, so much so that I instantly stopped talking, sensing she had something to say.

"You do know that we have no power in Thailand, abduction is not a crime here, and prostitution, I'm sorry to say, is the norm."

I did know all of that, "But what about the police?"

"The police have their own rules, I'm afraid. The best advice I can give you is not to go walking about on your own at night, stay in your hotel, only go to places you need to go to and most importantly keep out of trouble." She could tell I'd already dismissed her warnings. "Sean, I'm telling you now, if you try to kidnap your son back you will be charged," she said.

I didn't want to hear such negativity, it pained me to think of the barriers I was facing.

"I'll let the Ministry of Defence know what is going on and send them all the documentation," she continued, "Here's my mobile number, if anything happens just call me ,anytime, ok?"

"Thank you," I replied, shaking her hand before leaving the room.

As I walked back into the hotel, Paul spotted me and made his way over, "Did you have a good meeting?" he asked.

"Oh yes, it was fine," I said. The truth was I didn't have much else to report, "I'm just going up to my room; perhaps I'll catch you later?" I said trying to divert his questions once more.

"No problem, have a good day."

In my room I spread out all my paperwork on the bed and reminded myself just how far I had come; right, the next step, I thought, I need to book that flight to Chiang Mai. There was a flight going out the very next morning; I'd just taken another massive step towards my son.

Chapter 16 – United Nations

The following day I'd packed up all my belongings and was ready to start the next leg of my journey. "I'm checking out today," I said to Paul as I walked through the reception to the front desk.

"Already?" he said surprised.

"Yes, I'm going to Chiang Rai."

"You're travelling about then?"

"Yes mate, I've never been there before, fancied paying it a visit," I said vaguely.

"Chiang Rai's nice enough but don't forget to keep your eyes open," he said giving me a knowing look.

"Yes, I will don't worry, and thank you," I said realising that my eyes would be wide open, looking for my son.

"Here's my card, if you need me just give me a call."

"Yes I will thank you," I replied, grateful that there were some genuinely nice people in the world.

As I waited for my flight in the airport departure lounge I started to think of what I might find in Chang Rai; my worst fear up until then was that I wouldn't find him at all, but then I started to contemplate the possibility that I would find him, but I'd find him in a terrible state. I felt the colour drain from my cheeks, despite the scorching heat I felt icy cold at the thought that he was harmed or in pain somewhere. I looked out of the airport window, Thailand seemed like an alien place to me now, a country where I once felt at home, where I intended to live - it now seemed a cruel place. Had I really been that blinded by love, I questioned. And then I tried to remember the good times, tried to search for some sincerity in Kim's emotions, I couldn't tell anymore but I hoped that some of it was genuine.

My memories and my mind chatted away to me as I boarded the plane, glazing over the tunnel of smiling faces formed by the cabin crew. I endured the flight with an emotional pain in my stomach, I felt in mourning for the relationship that I thought I had and for the son that I hoped I'd have again.

On arrival Chiang Mai looked much the same as the other parts of Thailand I'd frequented. I took a minibus transfer to the hotel I'd booked, working my way around the city as my hotel was in fact the last drop off. I wasn't sure what to expect from my hotel but as the driver unloaded my case I felt pleasantly surprised. I walked into an ornately decorated foyer with walls adorned with pictures of happy tourists, previous guests of the hotel. Couples, families, lone travellers all seemed impressed with their choice and I too had a nice feeling about the place. The owners soon made themselves known to me, a Thai couple in their fifties very polite and with excellent English. The wife directed me to the check-in desk and I handed over my papers.

"I'm so sorry sir but you're at the wrong hotel, the driver has brought you to the wrong place." I rolled my eyes, when would something go right for me?

"I'll arrange a car to take you to your correct hotel, it's not too far."

"Ok, thank you," I said, starting to feel a bit grumpy.

"Do you want a drink and something to eat while you wait for the car?" she said.

"I'll have a drink please, but I can get a meal from the hotel after I've taken a shower, thank you anyway."

I sat down and her husband began to make the usual polite conversation, "Are you from England?"

"Yes."

139

"It's a very nice place," he said as if reminiscing.

"Have you been then?"

"Oh yes, many times, me and my wife have been all over the world, we go to the US a lot, my wife likes it there," he grinned lovingly in her direction.

"Oh right," I replied, "I haven't been to the US yet." And in that moment I suddenly felt relaxed as I realised that for the first time since I'd arrived back in Thailand, I felt safe. We chatted whilst I finished my drink and waited for my car to arrive. The couple walked me to the car door.

"If you're not happy with your hotel give us a call," the husband said as he passed me his business card, "We can arrange a car to pick you up again."

"Ok, thank you, and thank you for the drink!" I shouted before closing the car door behind me.

My actual hotel was only about 10 minutes away, it didn't ooze the welcoming atmosphere that my first drop off did, in fact it felt quite clinical but I was too tired to care. I went straight up to my room, showered and lay down on my bed relishing how close I was now. It was only a four hour drive to Chiang Rai; I'm so close now, I kept thinking to myself. I'd travelled thousands of miles and now I could almost allow myself to remember Joe's laugh again. I called home to let them know that I was safe and that everything was going ok, and then once again, slumber took hold and snatched me into a deep sleep.

I was woken early the following morning by the sound of the Islamic call to prayer. I rolled over with one eye open and squinted at my watch face; it was five a.m. I lay there trying to find my bearings and make sense of the droning prayers I could hear being blasted through a loud speaker. This was a whole new experience for me; I walked over to the hotel window

140

and looked out. The residents of Chiang Mai were busily getting ready for the day, it was still dark but people were moving to and fro, setting up market stalls and getting their business ready for a long day of trading. For a moment it amused me that the rest of the world were carrying on in blissful ignorance of Joe's plight; that I was cooped up in a hotel room thousands of miles from home, on a rescue mission that could change my life forever, and just metres below me women were literally arguing about the price of fish. And then I realised that these people rushing through the streets would be imitated almost identically back home in Cannock. The world over people were doing the same thing, getting ready for work, sending their children off to school, feeding their families; different colours and nations maybe but ultimately the same; and in that moment of realisation of equality I also realised that the world over there were good and bad. Kim truly belonged to the latter but I couldn't tar every Thai person with the same brush. I couldn't blame the whole nation for the failings of one person. Suddenly I was able to see Thailand as it was, the beautiful country filled with beautiful people; and my morning realisation empowered me for the rest of my quest.

Chapter 17 – So Close

After breakfast I decided to go and explore Chiang Mai; walking through the streets I started to plan the final leg of my journey. I would drive to Chiang Rai but I knew I had to get the timing absolutely right, I couldn't rush into it. I had one chance to find Joe and bring him back to the UK and everything in my body was telling me that a rash move could just blow it. I'd maintained contact with Kim via email, all the while pretending I will still shivering away in the UK, and she'd let slip that she wasn't with Joe. I'd already uncovered her life as a prostitute; I just didn't know where she was peddling her wares. Then it dawned on me; I froze; she could be right here. I could walk round the corner and be face to face with her, my story would be blown apart and Joe would be moved almost instantly. I turned and power-walked back to the hotel with my head down, praying that Kim was miles away. I got back to my room and quickly locked the door behind me; the sweat was beading off my forehead and I could hear my heart pounding. Once more I didn't feel safe, I felt for my wallet in my pocket and as I opened it up the card from the hotel I'd been mistakenly dropped off at yesterday peered out at me. I looked at it; I'd felt safe there; and without hesitation I dialled the number.

"Hello, this is Sean Felton; you gave me your card yesterday when I was taken to your hotel by mistake," I said hoping they'd remember me.

"Ah yes, the Englishman, how can I help you?" The male voice said.

"I'd like to come back and stay at your hotel if that's ok?"

"Yes you are very welcome; I'll send a car to pick you up."

Perfect I thought, and within minutes I'd packed up my belongings and was sitting waiting in the lobby.

As I neared the hotel I started to feel at peace again; I had no idea why but the vibes from the hotel worked well with me, they were calming.

"Mr Felton, you will enjoy your stay with us, we will make sure," the female owner said as she welcomed me from my car. And as I looked around once more, I truly believed that I would. My room didn't have all of the luxuries of the other hotel but it was clean and everyone was very friendly, and over the next couple of days I settled in and began to talk more openly about the reason for my trip.

It was on the third morning that I decided to take my briefcase and the treasured documents inside, down to breakfast. The hotel owners were chatting by the entrance to the kitchen.

"Excuse me, I was wondering if I could have a word with you once all of the breakfasts have finished?"

"Yes sure," she said looking slightly uncertain. "Is everything ok? Is your room ok?"

"Yes it's lovely, thank you. I just need to discuss something with you; the reason why I'm here in Thailand." The woman looked at me uneasily as if I'd just announced I was a foreign spy.

"It's all ok, don't worry," I clarified with a smile to break the difficult air.

The couple couldn't clear the breakfast things fast enough, their curiosity clearly consuming them. They sat down at my table and I brushed off the few crumbs that were spotted across the white tablecloth, before pulling the documents out of my briefcase and laying them in front of us. I started with a photograph, "This is my son," I said, opening my eyes wide to force back the tears. "As you can see he looks very happy."

"He is beautiful," the woman said, tilting her head to appreciate him further.

"Yes, thank you, he is." Then I pulled out a second photo, the one that Kim had sent through the post when he'd first gone missing. The woman was visibly taken aback.

"As you can see, he's scared." She raised her hand to her mouth in horror.

"I need to find him; I haven't seen him or heard his voice for six months now. Please, I need you to help me." I paused to check that the couple were still following. "I'm only four hours away from him now but I need to do this right, one bad mistake and he will go for good, I know he will."

The man looked me straight in the eye, "We will help you, don't worry, we'll tell you everything you need to know and help you get to where you need to be."

The kindness of these two individuals was astonishing. At that moment I knew I'd made the right choice in coming back to them and I broke down in tears, of relief and momentary happiness.

"Right, I'll take you to a friend's shop, he will translate all of your documents into Thai," the man said, clearly feeling the need to move swiftly. On the way to the shop I filled the man in on the rest of my story and he listened attentively, shaking and nodding his head in all the right places as I spoke. It was cathartic to retell the tale, and I hoped that it was soon to have a happy ending.

Walking into his friend's shop I stood in silence while my companion and his friend conversed in Thai for some time. I wondered what they were saying, hoping they weren't trying to con me, or unravel my plans in anyway. Eventually they stopped talking and the shop owner took my papers and walked through a small door towards the back of the shop.

"It's ok; we can come back for them tomorrow. Everything will be ok Sean, I promise."

I trusted him, I had to, and I duly walked away and got back in the car to go back to the hotel.

As we drove I started to feel uncomfortable, the heat that was previously annoying was now almost painful, burning me from the inside out. I felt lightheaded and my stomach started to talk to me in a language all of its own.

"Are you ok?" my new friend and driver asked.

"I don't feel too good," I said, realising something was terribly wrong.

"You don't look it. I'll call you a doctor when we get back to the hotel."

We got back just in time for me to rush to the toilet to be sick; an occurrence that would be the norm for the next 24 hours.

The doctor advised me to stay in bed the next day; not that I had the energy to do anything else, but that meant that I was a whole day behind schedule by the time I was ready to face the world again. I felt frustrated and just wanted to get things moving.

"So what's the situation with my documents?" I asked the hotel owner.

"We can pick them up this morning Sean, I've arranged for a driver to take you over there first thing."

"Great, we're getting somewhere," I said, glad to be making positive steps forward.

"We've also arranged for the driver to take you to the police station in Chiang Rai, you'll need to take all the documents and put them on their desk."

"Wow, you have been busy."

"Listen carefully Sean, when you give them the documents you must demand that they take you to find your son."

"Ok," I said nervously.

"It's only a small police station, they might ask for some money." I'd expected that.

"Make sure they take you and agree a price with them ok?" the woman finished.

"I will, thank you," I said.

"Please call us if you need our help again," the woman said, leaning in to give me a much needed warm hug of encouragement. Then she stepped back, pressed her hands together and bowed her head slightly, "I'll pray to Buddha for you, be safe."

"Thank you," I replied, touched by the gesture. "It's my son that needs the prayers, I'll be ok." I walked away to the waiting car to begin my journey to Chiang Rai. I didn't follow the route at all, I was too busy remembering Joe; reminiscing joyfully, and dreaming about the times to come once I'd found him. I smiled as I remembered him cheekily dancing to the music in the kitchen back home, he loved to dance, even when he was sitting down, if the radio came on he'd have to wiggle or bounce in some manner; he couldn't help himself. The driver sensed my thoughtful mood was because of Joe.

"You are going to find your son; don't worry," he said timidly.

"Thank you, I just hope he's ok. Child abduction is the most evil crime anyone can commit; she's not with him you know, he's on his own."

146

"Don't worry, sir," the driver said, "He'll be ok."

"I hope so," I said thinking that was the end of the conversation.

"But you do know it's the police you'll need to concentrate on, don't you?" I looked at him questioningly. "You have to make them take you; in this country your wife has done nothing wrong."

"I know," I said frustrated.

"You mustn't shout at them, don't make them think you are a ferrang."

"A what?"

"A foreigner. They must know that you are a good person and your son is in danger."

"Ok, I will; thank you."

"Don't make them angry, whatever you do, please don't make them angry, you don't want to end up in a Thailand jail," he looked at me sharply, "With white skin like yours, you'll die in there."

"Ok," I said slightly shaken by the reality check, "I understand." I knew what I had to do, but my plan wasn't driven by a desire to protect myself it was a desire to get Joe home; I just needed to find him.

We continued the rest of the journey in silence; pulling up outside the police station the driver got out of the car, I looked out of the window for a moment, staring at the station, wondering what fate lay in store once I went inside. I gathered up my bags, got out and shook the driver's hand. I was about to walk away, "Wait," he said before reaching back for my hand and proceeding to tie a white band around my wrist. Holding my wrist he then began to pray. I appreciated his prayers; I wasn't sure of what he said but when he'd finished he looked me in the eye and slowly smiled. I felt comforted.

"So long Sean, I wish you luck," he said before getting back in the car and driving away. I was on my own now. And as I walked up the steps to the entrance to the police station I tried desperately to remember all of the good advice that so many people had given me. I pushed open the heavy glass door and walked in. There were several men standing chatting in front of the main desk. They weren't in uniform but the way they eyeballed me told me immediately that they were policemen, and they looked like they wanted my blood. Play this cool Sean, I thought to myself, suddenly remembering my driver's advice in particular; don't make them angry. One policeman stepped forward, "Can I help you?" he said, looking me up and down.

"Yes," my voice cracked as I spoke. I stooped to put down my bags while I cleared my throat, "I hope so anyway." I opened my briefcase and started to put all the documents on the desk, "I need your help so I can find my son." But as soon as I started talking I felt everyone around me drift into their own conversations. I was stunned. They talked among themselves pointing at various pieces of my paperwork, occasionally one would pick up a sheet and pass it to a colleague; there was confusion, constant chattering; this wasn't how I'd imagined it. I hadn't even told them my story yet.

"Come with me," one of the more senior looking men said, walking over to his desk, "Name?" he said, drawing out a pen from his top pocket. Finally I'm getting somewhere, I thought. I started to tell my story, as I'd imagined I would, careful not to offend, not to say the wrong thing, and just as I got to the point where I would ask for their help, I was interrupted.

"We can't help you."

"What do you mean you can't help me? You have to; I've come a long way to find my son."

"Is your story big in the UK?" he asked.

"Yes, I have everyone involved, the media's eyes are on Thailand," I said, not sure if I was pushing my luck or not. He just looked at me.

"What about Interpol?" he questioned further.

"Yes, they're involved." I gulped hard.

"I am Interpol," he said laughing cruelly in my face.

"If you don't help me I will find him myself, I will go out there and track him down but if I get lost or something happens to me," I paused wondering whether I was sealing my fate, "Well, you'll have the world on your doorstep wanting to know what's become of me."

He didn't seem impressed by my half hearted threats but I had nothing to lose; he'd already stated he wouldn't help. He slowly got up from his chair and walked towards his colleagues who were still huddled over the desk full of papers. They conversed for a few moments and then he turned round to face me, now sweating profusely and feeling faint with anxiety.

"Ok," he said casually, "You take us out for a drink and some food and fill our police car with gasoline and we'll look for you."

"Yes that's absolutely fine," I said, finding the sudden change of heart and their humble request almost laughable. I'd expected them to ask me to hand over my life savings, not that I had any now, getting this far had left me with very little. Three of the men clambered towards the back room, and one by one they came out wearing their full police uniforms. As they filed pass me to collect their guns I became uncomfortably aware of their power and their reputed ruthlessness.

"Come with us," the senior officer said sternly. Not the usual way I get invited out for a drink, I thought to myself, trying desperately to stay calm. We walked outside and they each put their guns into the foot wells of the car.

"Get in," the shortest of the men said. I did as I was told. Sat in the back the guy to my right was talking into a mobile phone; I had no idea what he was saying or who to, but I knew he wasn't giving the caller much time to speak. I wondered if he was talking about Joe, if they knew something they weren't telling me. We jolted into motion as we drove away from the station.

"How far is it?" I said trying to keep the lines of communication open.

"We don't know," the driver offered, "This address could mean anything, it's right on the border of the golden triangle, even if we get close we might have trouble finding him."

Not what I wanted to hear, I hadn't come this far just to accept I couldn't find him. I would find him.

The terrain changed, the road become less uniform, resulting in me jostling on the back seat as the driver sped over bumps and through ditches. I tried my best to stay still, not wanting to irritate the policemen who flanked me. After a few minutes we slowed right down, I leaned forward to see where we were, hoping we'd reached our destination but it was just a police road block. I looked on curiously as we were waved through. Just moments later we came across another road block; the police were in the process of dragging two men from a beaten up old car they'd called over to the side of the road. I wasn't sure I wanted to see what they were going to do so I dipped my eyes to remain ignorant. Every other mile we encountered more of the same.

"Why are there so many police around?" I asked to anyone that would answer.

"It's very dangerous here," the driver said.

"People bring things through here," the guy in the passenger seat turned his head back slightly to address me but clearly wasn't going to elaborate further.

We drove for about an hour before turning off down a dirt track, the night was drawing in but I could clearly see that we were actually driving into the jungle. I started to feel uneasy; I wasn't sure if I could trust them, the conversation had dried up several miles back and only a few grunts in Thai were exchanged between the men who were otherwise silent and motionless.

Twenty minutes into the jungle and the car stopped. Each of the policemen opened their doors and got out; about to do the same I started to shuffle across to the open door. The policeman's face filled the black space, "Stay there," he said, shutting the door in my face.

I watched with my face up against the window, my hands cupped round my eyes to help me focus and tap into any night vision abilities I might possess. The men walked up to a hut. Is that where Joe is I thought to myself; every bone in my body wanted to fling the door open and raid the hut myself but something made me find some self restraint. Come on, come on I willed, watching the faint outlines of the men. One turned to come back towards me; my heart raced.

"Come with us," he ordered as he held the door for my exit.

He walked with me to the hut; I wanted to ask a thousand questions but instead I frantically licked my lips trying to find some moisture in my arid mouth. As I walked up to the doorway I noticed a well dressed man, scanning some of my papers. I tried to follow their Thai discussion and somehow I managed to ascertain that he was a police officer, who presumably living in this part of the country would be able to help us locate Joe.

151

Suddenly all eyes were on me, "Come, come with us," one said.

We were off again, back in the car. Every so often I felt like we were driving with purpose, like they knew exactly where they were heading, but then as I scanned the faces in the car the phrase 'wild goose chase' couldn't help but spring to mind. We drove for about another half an hour before we entered into a village, it was getting dark, as I peered into the blackness I could see that the huts were run down, some of them barely classifiable as homes. As we went by I was intensely aware of eyes watching us, discreetly at first but as we made our way along the makeshift road more and more faces appeared almost standing in guard of their homes. The car stopped abruptly and the police all stepped out in unison. The village spectators were growing in their numbers but the air was deadly silent. I slowly stepped out of the car; not sure whether I'd be safer there or by the side of the policemen, I hovered awkwardly in between the two. The driver was now talking to a small lady, hunched with age and frail in her frame. I watched intently as they spoke and then as she slowly raised her right hand and pointed a slender finger towards a hut on the opposite side of the track. My body went cold as I remembered the medium's exact words about a finger pointing towards a wooden hut. This is it, I thought, eyes wide, heart stopping and starting at will. And then I heard the words I never thought I'd hear.

"We've found your son."

I could feel my heart and soul rushing towards the hut the woman had pointed to but when I looked down I realised my emotions had left me paralysed.

"Come on Mr Felton," the youngest policeman said, tugging my arm slightly to remind me I had to move.

We walked towards the hut that now shone like a beacon in the night as police surrounded it, aiming flashlights and guns in hoards. I stood at the bottom of the broken wooden steps before slowly counting my way up them; feeling like the only way I could contain myself. I'd reached the door; I pushed it open, and there in front of me stood my wife.

"Where's Joe; where is he?" I blasted, rage boiling in my gut. She bowed her head and without saying a word pointed to another door towards the back of the house. I pushed past her, opened the door, and cried. There, huddled in the corner of the room, looking scared and dishevelled was my holy grail; my son. I wiped the gushing tears from my eyes to focus on him properly; he was shaking, seemingly finding comfort in the apple he was clutching for dear life. I slowly dropped down onto my knees, aware that I didn't want to scare him anymore, and offered my hands out to him. He looked into my eyes and with one powerful gaze he found that bond. He pulled himself to his feet and cautiously started to walk towards me. I felt like the room was spinning.

"Come on Jobie, I won't hurt you," I said, so grateful that I'd gotten the chance to speak to him again. He cautiously lifted up his arms towards me and I swept him up into mine, pulling him close into my heart. I pulled my head back to take him in; to cherish his face and as I did he leant forward and kissed me. I wept.

"You're safe now, you're safe Jobie; no one's going to hurt you anymore," I sobbed.

His smile took my breath away; a sight I never thought I'd see again. With my legs trembling I carried him outside in my arms, standing at the top of the steps

I looked down at the sea of eyes staring back; the villagers had come out in their droves.

"I've got him," I shouted, looking down at my son in my arms; my love for him almost suffocating me. He smiled again, and then I noticed that his smile wasn't as I remembered; his front teeth were broken and as I ran my hands across his face arms and legs I noticed many things that weren't as I remembered. Things that painfully gave me an insight into what my poor boy had been through. The fingertips on one hand looked sore and ragged; and then I realised that his finger nails had been ripped out. I kissed his hand and in lifting his arm to do so I spotted the bruises. I felt sick.

"What have you done to him?" Kim just looked at me, chillingly emotionless. I walked away in disgust, down the wooden steps still cradling Joe in my arms; I wasn't going to let him go again.

"You have to come with us back to Chiang Rai now and leave your son here," one of the policemen said calmly.

"What? What do you mean?" I said bemused, "What are you saying; she'll run with him, I'll never find him," I couldn't believe what I was hearing; I hadn't trekked across the world to have a five minute cuddle; I wanted to take Joe home.

"You're coming back with us," the policeman repeated. How could this be happening, I thought, I've only just got him back and these crazy men are asking me to leave him here; I just looked at them, my face explaining exactly what I was thinking.

"Don't worry, she's going nowhere," one of them said, "My friend is staying in the village, she can't leave," he continued confidently.

"I'm sorry but I've been looking for my son for six months and you just want me to leave him?"

"You have no choice," he said abruptly. "We'll bring you back in the morning, come, come."

I reluctantly got back in the car; every inch of me was fighting it but the flash of gun barrels overruled my heart. I looked out at Joe, standing timidly, looking even more lost than when I'd walked in just minutes earlier. My poor, poor boy, I thought, hoping he could somehow know for certain that I'd be back for him. I watched him as the car pulled away, fixing my eyes on his until his perfect silhouette merged with the night sky and his face was once again a memory.

Chapter 18 – A Deal with the Devil

"She's only been back two days," the policeman in the passenger seat said, looking back over his shoulder.

"Really?"

"Yes, the lady in the village told me."

"I knew she hadn't been there with him," I said.

"You were right Sean," he said, the formalities fading away, "Your son has been kept away from the people in the village so they wouldn't talk, so she wouldn't be caught."

"But that lady knew where he was?" I questioned.

"Yes she knew."

Thank God, I thought to myself.

Suddenly the darkness turned from charcoal to opaque black, I peered out through the window glass, there weren't any street lights; we were once again entering the jungle, either side of us trees were stretching up and filling the sky with branches and foliage. As I stared out I tried to understand my feelings; I'd just found my boy and been forced to abandon him again, and now here I was driving through potentially dangerous jungle to who knows where. I felt fearful, confused, relieved.

"We're nearly back in Chiang Rai," the driver said, interrupting my thoughts.

"Time for that drink then," another continued.

I'd forgotten all about my promise to wine and dine them, but they'd kept their part of the bargain, they'd helped me find Joe, so I had to fulfil my part. And so it was that I found myself as an extra on a Thai policemen's night out. They drank heavily, and laughed and joked together while I sat at the end of the table getting lost in translation, feeling drained and uncomfortable. I tried my best to be polite and make sure they were having a good time, but my thoughts were very much elsewhere, they were back in that hut, with my wide eyed boy, covered in bruises. The night came to an end at around midnight, and I was thankful when the last of the policemen staggered off into the distance, leaving me free to return to my hotel.

I didn't sleep that night, every time I closed my eyes I saw his face, and I analysed every moment of our all too brief reunion; had he instantly recognised me? Had he forgotten me? Did he think I'd left him again? The unanswerable questions kept swimming around my head until 7 a.m. when my slightly hung-over entourage met me at the front of the hotel to drive back to the village. We drove in silence, my companions clearly suffering the effects of the excesses of the night before. I took the opportunity to catch up on my sleep; I knew I needed to be on top form to stay abreast of whatever legalities would be occurring today, so I closed my eyes and drifted away.

The car came to a steady halt. I rubbed my eyes to take in my surroundings; we were back at the police station. I took a deep breath before walking up the stairs and into the main door. And there, sat innocently between Kim and her sister, was Joe.

"Hello Jobie," I said my heart pulling me towards him.

He made some noises but I didn't recognise them at words, English or Thai.

In the daylight he looked even more unfortunate than I'd noticed the night before. He looked pale, withdrawn, weak. I glared at Kim, unable to find the words to express my disgust. I tickled him and a smile slowly formed in the corners of his mouth. A few moments later he managed a real laugh. I didn't think a noise so simple could be so powerful. I almost felt my heart start beating again.

As he tried to engage with our game some more it was clear that he couldn't speak anything other than jibber jabber, a mixture of noises and grunts, but the language of laughter was clearly universal.

"Mr Felton, come this way please," an unfamiliar policeman said.

I stood up, feeling as though I'd been called to the headmaster's office. Taking Joe by the hand I walked in and sat down in one of the large desk chairs. I swept him up and put him on my lap. "We have something to tell you," the policeman said solemnly; I braced myself for some bad news.

"English laws don't mean anything in Thailand; this is not your country, what your wife has done, well this is no crime in Thailand."

"You what?" I was outraged. "Look at him; does he look healthy to you? Look what they've done to him," I said, raising up his battered arms. The policeman on the other side of the desk just shook their heads.

"Your wife's sister said she wants him to live with her; you can send money for your son from England."

"Is that all you lot think about! He's not something that can be sold, he's *my* son, they're not having him; he's my son and they're not going anywhere near him." The strength of my bond with Joe lit the spark in my belly that sent the words blasting out like fireworks. "What do you want, for her to go off working as a prostitute looking for her next victim, while he lives in a shed?" I was fuming. "God knows what they've done to him!" I put Joe down on the floor beside my chair, as one of the men approached me; his face moved in just centimetres from my own.

"Well it'll have to go to court in Chiang Rai," he whispered with a smirk. I laughed at his effort, "Listen to me, do you think I'm stupid? I've looked at the Thai law and if it's going to court I want it to go the family courts in Bangkok."

"No way," the man said clearly shocked by my request.

"What do you mean, no way? I'll contact the embassy and tell them what you're doing; this is wrong he's my child, you're not going to scare me into giving him back to them."

Kim stood up and finally spoke, "Stop it, stop it!" she shouted. "I want to talk to you," she said, directing it at the uniformed men. They began talking in Thai, I picked Joe up into my arms and walked him back out into the waiting area. With him sat snugly on my hip I looked into his face; despite the lifelessness in his eyes, he was perfection. The thought of leaving Thailand without him made me physically heave. Tears welled in my eyes as he started jabbering merrily and playing with the side of my face.

"Mr Felton!" I turned round to see a man beckoning me back into the interview room.

"You're one lucky man," he said, as I passed him on the way through the door.

"What do you mean?"

"You have to go with your wife and her family; they'll take you back to the hotel."

I looked at Kim bemused, "Ok," I said and did as I was told, walking outside and getting into the car with Joe held tightly on my lap. My mind was working overtime. The last forty eight hours had been so intense, with highs and lows and questions and answers; I didn't think I could take much more.

"Where are we going?" I said wearily noticing that we were driving in the opposite direction to the hotel.

"We have to get something," Kim said.

I wanted to declare how sick I was of the wild goose chase; I wanted to run for the hills with Joe in my arms but instead I kept quiet, sat still and watched the Thai countryside pass by the car window. We drove for about an hour before arriving in an unfamiliar village. What are they planning to do? I thought to myself. We pulled up outside a courtyard of four huts, Kim and her family got out of the car and walked into the largest hut directly in front of the car, which still had the engine running. Well we're obviously not stopping, I thought to myself but what on earth could she be getting?

Seconds later my question was answered as Kim walked back out with a pushchair and folded it up to put into the boot of the car. What does this mean I thought, my heart pounding as I dared to contemplate the best. We drove back to Chiang Rai in silence, and with Joe sleeping on my lap I took the time to enjoy my first long cuddle; the touch of his hair under my chin sent tingles down my spine. Suddenly the road looked familiar. We were nearing my hotel; I started to breath heavily as I panicked about what was to happen next. I climbed out of the car, Joe still dozing in my arms, and started to walk towards the hotel reception, Kim came alongside me;

"Don't say anything; I don't want it to go to the court, my family will disown me," she whispered as we walked side by side.

I stopped and looked straight at her; I had to play this cool, "So what are you thinking, Kim?"

"You can take him, but I want all the land and I want some more money; but you have to let me come

160

to the UK to visit now and again, oh, and I want full citizenship in the UK."

"Yes, fine," I said, "You can have all that, no problem." I sat down in the foyer, the weight of Joe was so drastically different to when I'd last carried him as a sleeping babe, and I couldn't hold him up when faced with such news. Kim stood in front of me, oblivious to the fact that in her long list of demands she was effectively selling her own child. I was repulsed; this woman that I once loved had just sold our child.

"Will England let me have the citizenship?" she asked with a sense of desperation.

"Oh yes," I said confidently, "It shouldn't be a problem; you lived there for a long time." I paused, "I'll tell you what I'll do, I'll call them and arrange a meeting in Bangkok." I pulled my phone out and began to dial the number; I saw Kim's eyes light up just as mine had done when I saw Joe. The number I was dialling was the number I was given when I first arrived in Thailand all those weeks ago.

"Hello, it's Sean Felton; we had a meeting about my abducted son."

"Ah yes, hello," the lady on the other end of the line said.

"Listen, I have to be quick, I've found my son and his mum has said I can take him back to the UK," I looked down at him now starting to wake up. "He's not in a good state and he really needs to be back in the UK," I adjusted my tone, "The only thing is, his mum wants a meeting, please tell her she's doing the right thing, she's just sold him back to me," I turned my back to Kim, "What kind of parent does that?" I whispered.

"Ok, book a flight back to Bangkok and I'll see you."

"Thank you so much," I said relieved that Kim would be at least partially satisfied.

I booked the flight and the three of us flew back to Bangkok together. I struggled to talk to Kim, the anger and resentment I harboured was not leaving me, even the slightest bit, despite having Joe back in my life. And Kim was untypically quiet; I presumed through guilt. But it didn't bother me, I could've happily chatted to Joe and Joe alone for the next twenty years of my life; I didn't feel like I needed anybody else.

"It's going to be me and you son," I whispered in his ear; a rapturous giggle was his reply.

At Bangkok Kim was afforded the meeting she'd requested and her demeanour afterwards suggested that it all went as she'd hoped. I didn't pry too much, I didn't want to risk upsetting her and her changing her mind about the twisted deal that she'd already brokered.

We made our way back to the hotel in Bangkok; to an outsider looking like a blissfully happy, perfect family of three; but to us on the inside it couldn't have been farther from the truth.

Walking along the hotel corridor, I could sense Kim had something to say so I stopped and looked into her eyes, "Well?"

"I want to stay with him for one week," she said, "Here in the hotel."

"Ok," I said calmly. One week was nothing if it meant I could take him back home with me at the end of it.

And so it was, that week I reacquainted myself with my precious son, I took care of him in a way that only a truly committed parent would. I took him to have his hair cut, so I could see his cheeky face properly, in all its glory rather than peering out from behind a mop of hair. I bought him new clothes to replace the tatty ones he'd been tolerating for goodness knows how long. And in just one week of my devotion he started to look better, healthier; he started to seem like a happy little boy once more. Each day I played with him in the pool, splashing and laughing, and with each second the time we'd spent apart seemed to diminish into just a moment. The whole week Kim made random requests and demands, for me to buy her things or take Joe to places. I agreed with it all. I'd had a taste of the life I'd been yearning; I knew this woman was crazy and capable of anything so I went out of my way to keep the peace.

And after a beautiful seven days the time came for me to take my boy back to the UK. I packed up all our belongings and organised a bag for hand luggage, full of toys and spare clothes for Joe. Kim just stared at us both in silence. She unsettled me; all I could think was that she was going to change her mind; I just needed to get through the next few hours and Joe and I would be on our way home. We made our way down to the front of the hotel to wait for the taxi I'd booked earlier that morning. Come on, come on, I willed in my head, whilst holding tightly onto Joe's hand. Both our hands were sweating profusely but I didn't dare let it drop. I was so, so close. The white taxi pulled up in front of us, "Felton?" the driver questioned through the open window.

I nodded, opened up the rear door and strapped Joe in; then I started to load my bags into the back, waiting for her to cause a scene, to ask for more money, to try and run away. In my head I could anticipate a grand, "I've fooled you," coming from her lips. But she remained silently dignified. She leant into the back of the cab to say her goodbyes, and as she stood up and closed Joe's door I noticed a solitary tear fall suddenly down her face. As the taxi pulled away I wondered whether that was a tear of sadness or guilt.

I looked down at Joe by my side and put my hand on his head; he looked up and smiled at me.

"I found you, son; I've got you back," I said, "You're going to see nanny and play with all your toys back in England," I said excitedly. He just smiled at me. And in that moment I felt complete again.

The airport check-in went smoothly, our bags were loaded onto the conveyer and I could tell that Joe loved the whole experience. Our flight was called;

"That's us!" I said scooping Joe up from where he was playing with his toys on the floor. We joined the queue of travellers waiting at passport control and Joe started to get restless, "Not long now, son," I said shuffling forward to meet the official on the desk. I showed him our passports; he looked at me, looked at Joe then spun his chair round to talk to one of his colleagues behind me. What's going on now, I worried. More looks were shot in our direction; I felt nervous.

"Come with me, sir," a policeman said appearing from nowhere behind me.

Oh no, this can't be happening I thought, my mouth instantly drying up at the thought that Joe and I wouldn't make it on the plane. We walked into a small, sparse room; just a battered old table with a chair on either side. He didn't offer me a seat so I chose not to take one, optimistic that I wouldn't be there long. The officer went straight over to the telephone and made a call, all the while flicking through our passports from cover to cover. His conversation was in Thai; I was listening intently but understanding nothing. Joe started to whinge, "its ok son, we won't be long now," I said hoping it was the truth.

The phone went down. The policeman looked at me, "Ok you can go."

"That's it?" I questioned.

"Yes, you're free to go."

I didn't question twice; I picked Joe up and ran down the corridor to find our seats on the waiting plane; we'd made it. And as I looked away from my excited little boy and looked out onto the disappearing landscape of Thailand I finally realised that my nightmare had ended.

Epilogue

But why did she do it? Your children are a part of you, your own flesh and blood; money shouldn't come into the value of a human life. If Joe had remained in Thailand he would either have been sold into the sex trade or grown up in poverty; Thailand was no place for him. When I brought Joe home I knew that he would be safe and that from that moment on he would have the best life I could give him. I knew it wouldn't be easy getting him back on a level, helping him to adjust back to life in the UK; he didn't speak properly and was very confused, but I'd got my son back and we were about to commence on a new adventure together. And now I will be able to see him grow into a man, watch him get married and have children of his own.

I went through the cruellest of pain and heartache in the search for him but the reward at the end, of being able to hold Joe in my arms and never again having to imagine if he were alive or dead, was ample compensation for my trauma. From that day forward I could see the miracle of life with my own eyes and I could kiss him goodnight; what more could a father ask for.

For any parent that has lost a child through parental abduction my heart goes out to you, I feel your pain. It is important to remember that although every abduction is different, they are all still crimes; the innocence of children should be respected; they shouldn't be used as a pawn between feuding couples or as bartering power for material goods, children deserve a good life, they deserve to be loved.

Lightning Source UK Ltd.
Milton Keynes UK
UKOW052207270612

195166UK00004B/3/P